Helping
TEENS
Handle Tough
Experiences

STRATEGIES TO FOSTER
RESILIENCE

JILL NELSON, Ph.D., and SARAH KJOS, M.Ed.

SEARCH
INSTITUTE
PRESS

Helping Teens Handle Tough Experiences:
Strategies to Foster Resilience

The following are registered trademarks of Search Institute: Search Institute® , Developmental Assets®, and

Jill Nelson, Ph.D and Sarah Kjos, M.Ed.

Search Institute Press, Minneapolis, MN
Copyright © 2008 by Search Institute

10 9 8 7 6 5 4 3 2 1
Printed on acid-free paper in the United States of America

Search Institute
615 First Avenue Northeast, Suite 125
Minneapolis, MN 55413
www.search-institute.org
612-376-8955 • 877-240-7251

ISBN-13: 978-1-57482-248-9
ISBN-10: 1-57482-248-9

Credits
Editors: Tenessa Gemelke, Kate Brielmaier
Book Design: Percolator
Production Supervisor: Mary Ellen Buscher

Library of Congress Cataloging-in-Publication Data
Nelson, Jill, Ph.D.
  Helping teens handle tough experiences : strategies to foster resilience / Jill Nelson and Sarah Kjos.
    p. cm.
  ISBN-13: 978-1-57482-248-9 (pbk. : alk. paper)
  ISBN-10: 1-57482-248-9 (pbk. : alk. paper)
  1. Social work with teenagers. 2. Resilience (Personality trait) in adolescence. I. Kjos, Sarah. II. Title.
  HV1421.N44 2008
  362.7—dc22   2008007154

About Search Institute Press

Search Institute Press is a division of Search Institute, a nonprofit organization that offers leadership, knowledge, and resources to promote positive youth development. Our mission at Search Institute Press is to provide practical and hope-filled resources to help create a world in which all young people thrive. Our products are embedded in research, and the 40 Developmental Assets®—qualities, experiences, and relationships youth need to succeed—are a central focus of our resources. Our logo, the SIP flower, is a symbol of the thriving and healthy growth young people experience when they have an abundance of assets in their lives.

Licensing and Copyright

Printing Tips

To produce high-quality copies of activity sheets for distribution without spending a lot of money, follow these tips:

- Always copy from the original. Copying from a copy lowers the reproduction quality.

- Make copies more appealing by using brightly colored paper or even colored ink. Quick-print shops often run daily specials on certain colors of ink.

- For variety, consider printing each activity sheet on a different color of paper.

- If you are using more than one activity sheet or an activity sheet that runs more than one page, make two-sided copies.

CONTENTS

INTRODUCTION

Teens can experience significant difficulties in their lives. Adversity can set up barriers to a teen's success, making it imperative that we work with youth to help them build on their natural talents, goodness, and strengths. In doing this, we must not minimize the painful and even frightening times youth may go through; rather, we must seek to better understand each teen's experience, educate ourselves on the issues youth face, and play a role in being a positive influence in their lives.

The difficulties that confront youth may stem from the family, society, the individual, or a combination of sources. Removing the adversity from a young person's life may be beyond our capabilities, but we *can* influence positive change for individuals and society. The more knowledge we have about specific obstacles teens must deal with, the better equipped we are to work with youth we encounter. The ideas in this book are practical strategies we can integrate into our work to better serve teens living with challenging experiences.

Every young person responds differently to adversity. This response may be based on many factors, including the young person's support system (whether it is healthy and helpful or dysfunctional and harmful), his connection to the community and its services, and his self-worth. Most teenagers respond to and cope with adversity the best they can, based on the skills they've learned and the people in their lives. Adversity does not define a teen, nor does it preclude him from achieving his potential as a child or an adult. Most youth are doing the best they can with what they have.

ABOUT THIS BOOK

This book highlights 20 "tough experiences," or adversities—many of which have a direct relationship to one another (for example, a youth who has been sexually abused may employ self-injury as an ineffective coping mechanism). These topics do not provide an exhaustive overview of the challenges youth face, but they do reflect many of the most pressing issues youth are dealing with in your community. These topics were chosen based on issues repeatedly identified through conversations with youth service providers, members of the educational community, and the authors' own experiences working with youth.

Each chapter in this book discusses a different challenge that a teen may face. For every challenge, you'll find an overview of the topic and an exploration of the ways in which it might affect youth. That is followed by a "What You Can Do to Help" section, which provides practical advice, tips, and suggestions for working with teens who are dealing with these challenges. Each chapter also includes reproducible handouts to give to other educators and youth workers, parents, or teens themselves, and contains suggestions for further reading, Web sites, and contact information for relevant organizations. From time to time you'll see sidebars containing quotes from teens about the experiences they have faced. These quotes were collected through interviews and discussions facilitated by the authors, and the teens' names have been changed to protect their privacy.

LEGAL RESPONSIBILITIES

If you are reading this book, chances are you are what is called a "mandated reporter." A mandated reporter is someone who is legally obligated to report suspected child abuse or neglect. In most states, a person who has regular interactions with children as a part of her or his employment is a mandated reporter. In other states, every person is considered a mandated reporter. In either case, it is important to know your state laws regarding when you are obligated or mandated to report child abuse or neglect. Many of the issues in this book fall under the umbrella of mandated reporting. The specific process for making such a report varies by state and agency, so it is best to seek advice from a local trusted source, such as a school counselor or social worker. Typically, these people are trained in such matters and deal with them on a regular basis.

People sometimes agonize over whether to report what they have observed. Many states allow anonymous reporting, and keep in mind that when you report suspected abuse or neglect, you are only calling to report your suspicions or what you saw. Someone else will make the determination about what course of action, if any, needs to be taken. In some cases, you will be one of many people who have called about the same youth. It is also important to know that the legal consequences (as well as the moral consequences) of not reporting suspected abuse or neglect are often severe.

SEEKING FURTHER RESOURCES

Helping Teens Handle Tough Experiences is not designed to provide comprehensive care for youth, but rather to serve as a resource and a starting point. Whether you are a teacher working with a student you are concerned for, a mentor to a teenager living in a dangerous environment, or simply a concerned adult, you may find yourself in a situation that is difficult to navigate. It is vital to connect youth with professional counseling, treatment, and supportive services when needed.

STRENGTH INTERVIEWING

Talking to teens can be a challenge, especially when they are facing adversity. This brief chapter gives an overview of a method that some professionals call *strength interviewing*. The basic premise of a strength interview is to inquire about a teen's positive influences or attributes, and to build on them. Adolescents may have many adults in their lives who lecture them and tell them what to do. A strength-based approach to talking to teens empowers them and can leave them feeling better about themselves, not worse. When you are discussing difficult issues with a teen, it is important not only to talk about the problem but also to discuss the specific strengths that a teen has. These resources can be used to tackle the problems he faces.

Strength interviewing focuses on what a teen can do, not what she can't do; on what a teen is doing well, not what she is doing poorly; on what is right, not what is wrong. Strength interviewing doesn't ignore the problem, but instead balances problem-talk with solution-talk. Hear the teen out. Let her talk about the problem, and, when it is appropriate, help her build a solution with you. Solution building should be a collaborative effort, not an opportunity for you to tell a teen what to do.

While conducting interviews, one skill is most important: listening. Many teens don't like talking to adults because some adults tend not to listen, and may be quick to offer advice or a scolding. When teens are in trouble they are usually aware that what they are doing is wrong, or is going against what is expected of them; they don't need another person to focus on the negative aspects of their behavior. Listening to a teen's problems and echoing or repeating back what you have heard is a good way to know if you understand what he has just shared with you. When you do comment, use phrases such as "It sounds like you're saying . . ." or "Let me make sure I'm hearing what you mean." If you don't get it right the first time, continue listening and reflecting until the teen feels understood.

Search Institute, a nonprofit group that studies child and adolescent development, has created a list of 40 strengths, or Developmental Assets, that a youth needs to grow and thrive. Refer to the section on Developmental Assets, beginning on page 7, to see if there are strengths that the teen may have overlooked. Strength interviews are very much in line with the Developmental Assets approach, and the assets can help you find out what is "going right" for the teen.

Once you understand the problem, assist the teen in working out a solution. Each chapter has guidance about resources and when to seek professional help. Use these resources and inquire about which strengths each teen has. Build on these strengths and look for additional resources to help conquer the problem at hand.

This idea is simple in theory, but it may take lots of practice to do well. Teens are worth the effort—help them build their strengths!

Strength Interviewing Tips

- Understand the problem—*listen* and *reflect* what you heard.

- Don't give advice, scold, or lecture—be a person in a teen's life who doesn't do this.

- Understand emotions as well as events. Make sure you connect with a teen's feelings.

- Inquire about what is "going right" for the teen. What assets does he have that can help him build a strategy for the situation?

- Think about the 40 Developmental Assets® on pages 10 and 11. Are there assets the teen may have overlooked?

- Bearing in mind the strategies provided in each of the chapters, build a strength-based and asset-focused plan of intervention.

Suggestions for
Strength Interview Questions

General Strength Questions

When do you most feel like you can be yourself?

What do you do that helps you cope with distress? What ideas do you have for other things you could try to help you cope?

What are you doing to take care of yourself emotionally?

What healthy strategies do you find most helpful in releasing emotions?

What helps you feel strong and capable in this situation?

What environments or settings do you feel most comfortable in?

What helps you feel safe?

When do you feel connected to your peers and the community?

Who are the adults who treat you with respect?

Who is an adult you can turn to when you feel sad, angry, or resentful toward your parents?

Who has been the most influential person in your life?

Where can you turn when you need emotional support?

Who has been supportive as you work through your concerns?

If you don't feel supported by the people in your life, what opportunities do you have to connect with other caring people?

Strength Questions for Addressing Abuse:

Who has been supportive and understands that the abuse was not your fault?

What have you done to help yourself cope with the abuse?

What are other positive things you could try to do to help yourself cope?

What have you done or are you doing to increase your personal safety?

If you have a parent who is being victimized, how do you find additional support for yourself?

CONTINUES →

Strength Questions for Addressing Addiction:

What are all the possible scenarios that could happen the next time you use chemicals?

If you use again, how will you get home safely? If you feel unsafe or know you need to leave, who can you call to take you home?

What can you do to feel independent without chemical use?

What is the worst thing that could happen if you cut down on your chemical use or quit using? What is the best thing that could happen?

What information on chemical use and abuse would be helpful to you?

Who is supportive and understanding in your life and lets you know you are not to blame for your parent being an addict?

Strength Questions for Changes in Living Situation:

What will help you cope with your transition to a new setting?

You may have lost some things in your life in this transition. Can you think of the things you've lost and gained?

How could you express your perspective on foster care and your experiences being part of foster care? (Suggestions of portable things teens can take with them: art, journaling, poetry, photography, etc.).

What do you want people to know about homelessness?

THE 40 DEVELOPMENTAL ASSETS

What does it mean to be strength-based? Search Institute, a nonprofit research group, has identified 40 strengths that teens can draw on. The 40 Developmental Assets describe qualities and experiences that are crucial to positive youth development. They range from external supports like a caring school climate and positive family communication to internal characteristics such as school engagement and a sense of purpose.

Search Institute has done extensive research, reviewing more than 1,200 studies from major bodies of literature, including prevention, resilience, and adolescent development, to identify what young people need to thrive. Institute researchers have documented that young people who are healthy, whether they come from the poorest or the wealthiest environments and from diverse ethnic and cultural groups, have certain meaningful elements in their lives. Researchers identified eight categories that describe these elements:

- The solid presence of **support** from others;

- A feeling of **empowerment**;

- A clear understanding of **boundaries and expectations**;

- Varied opportunities for **constructive use of time**;

- A strong **commitment to learning**;

- An appreciation of **positive values**;

- Sound **social competencies**; and

- A personal sense of **positive identity**.[1, 2]

Moreover, research conducted by Search Institute consistently shows that the strengths described within these categories provide a solid foundation for positive development and academic success, and that their presence helps protect youth from engaging in risky behavior and promotes youth acting in productive ways. The institute identified 40 different components and gave the name "Developmental Assets" to these building blocks of healthy youth development. The data consistently show that the power of assets is cumulative: The more assets young people report experiencing, the more apt they are to succeed in school and live positive lives, and the less likely they are to participate in high-risk behaviors such as drug use, violence, and early sexual activity.

The Power of Assets

On one level, the 40 Developmental Assets represent common wisdom about the kinds of positive experiences and characteristics that young people need and deserve. But their value extends further. Surveys of more than 2 million young people in grades 6–12 have shown that assets are powerful influences on adolescent behavior. (The numbers below reflect 2003 data from 148,189 young people in 202 communities.) Regardless of gender, ethnic heritage, economic situation, or geographic location, these assets both promote positive behaviors and attitudes and help protect young people from many different problem behaviors.

0–10 ASSETS   11–20 ASSETS   21–30 ASSETS   31–40 ASSETS

PROMOTING POSITIVE BEHAVIORS AND ATTITUDES

Search Institute research shows that the greater the number of assets students report having, the more likely they are to also report the following patterns of thriving behavior:

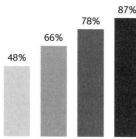

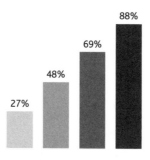

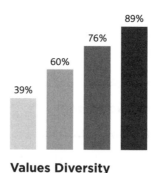

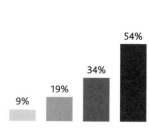

Exhibits Leadership
Has been a leader of an organization or group in the past 12 months.

Maintains Good Health
Takes good care of body (such as eating foods that are healthy and exercising regularly).

Values Diversity
Thinks it is important to get to know people of other racial/ethnic groups.

Succeeds in School
Gets mostly A's on report card (an admittedly high standard).

PROTECTING YOUTH FROM HIGH-RISK BEHAVIORS

Assets not only promote positive behaviors, they also protect young people; the more assets a young person reports having, the less likely he or she is to make harmful or unhealthy choices. (Note that these definitions are set rather high, suggesting ongoing problems rather than experimentation.)

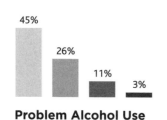

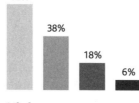

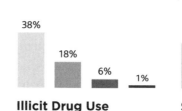

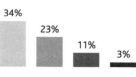

Problem Alcohol Use
Has used alcohol three or more times in the past 30 days or got drunk once or more in the past two weeks.

Violence
Has engaged in three or more acts of fighting, hitting, injuring a person, carrying a weapon, or threatening physical harm in the past 12 months.

Illicit Drug Use
Used illicit drugs (marijuana, cocaine, LSD, PCP or angel dust, heroin, or amphetamines) three or more times in the past 12 months.

Sexual Activity
Has had sexual intercourse three or more times in lifetime.

USING THE ASSETS TO FOSTER RESILIENCE

Everyone has assets. Teens who lack a stable family life may have positive relationships at school; youth struggling in the classroom may have strong connections with their community. If someone is lacking assets in one area, he or she still has many other opportunities for strength—and identifying and supporting those opportunities can make a great deal of difference to a teen facing a crisis.

The term "resilience" in this book refers to the ability to cope in the face of adversity. Building resilience doesn't mean removing all adversity, but rather increasing one's ability to face and overcome the challenges life brings. Using the Developmental Assets and the positive, strength-based approach described in this book will help the teens you are working with overcome adversity and build resilience.

When you conduct strength-based interviews, it can be helpful to use the list of Developmental Assets as a guide for finding the positive characteristics in a teen's life. Use them to inspire strength-interview questions, such as:

Who are the caring adults in your life?

How does your creativity help you handle your emotions?

Where do you feel safe?

What makes you feel confident about yourself?

Where are you when you feel most comfortable,
or when this feels least like a problem for you?

Once you have identified these positive opportunities, you can work with the teen on emphasizing and enhancing them. Suggest ways to connect with caring adults. Encourage creativity. Help ensure access to safe places. Maintaining a strength-based focus while problem solving is a positive approach to building resilience. Helping a teen through her problems while building resilience not only helps her with the problem at hand but also helps her build coping skills that she can carry with her into the future. Youth who are facing difficulties in one area of life can find strength and comfort in realizing that they have support in other parts of their lives, and can still be successful in other ways.

NOTES

1. Peter C. Scales and Nancy Leffert, *Developmental Assets: A Synthesis of the Scientific Research on Adolescent Development*, 2d ed. (Minneapolis: Search Institute, 2004).

2. Peter C. Scales, Arturo Sesma, Jr., and Brent Bolstrom, *Coming into Their Own: How Developmental Assets Promote Positive Growth in Middle Childhood* (Minneapolis: Search Institute, 2004).

The Framework of 40 Developmental Assets® for Adolescents

Search Institute has identified the following building blocks of healthy development that help young people grow up healthy, caring, and responsible.

EXTERNAL ASSETS

SUPPORT

1. **Family Support**—Family life provides high levels of love and support.

2. **Positive Family Communication**—Young person and her or his parent(s) communicate positively, and young person is willing to seek advice and counsel from parent(s).

3. **Other Adult Relationships**—Young person receives support from three or more nonparent adults.

4. **Caring Neighborhood**—Young person experiences caring neighbors.

5. **Caring School Climate**—School provides a caring, encouraging environment.

6. **Parent Involvement in Schooling**—Parent(s) are actively involved in helping young person succeed in school.

EMPOWERMENT

7. **Community Values Youth**—Young person perceives that adults in the community value youth.

8. **Youth as Resources**—Young people are given useful roles in the community.

9. **Service to Others**—Young person serves in the community one hour or more per week.

10. **Safety**—Young person feels safe at home, at school, and in the neighborhood.

BOUNDARIES AND EXPECTATIONS

11. **Family Boundaries**—Family has clear rules and consequences and monitors the young person's whereabouts.

12. **School Boundaries**—School provides clear rules and consequences.

13. **Neighborhood Boundaries**—Neighbors take responsibility for monitoring young people's behavior.

14. **Adult Role Models**—Parent(s) and other adults model positive, responsible behavior.

15. **Positive Peer Influence**—Young person's best friends model responsible behavior.

16. **High Expectations**—Both parent(s) and teachers encourage the young person to do well.

CONSTRUCTIVE USE OF TIME

17. **Creative Activities**—Young person spends three or more hours per week in lessons or practice in music, theater, or other arts.

18. **Youth Programs**—Young person spends three or more hours per week in sports, clubs, or organizations at school and/or in the community.

19. **Religious Community**—Young person spends one or more hours per week in activities in a religious institution.

20. **Time at Home**—Young person is out with friends "with nothing special to do" two or fewer nights per week.

CONTINUES →

INTERNAL ASSETS

COMMITMENT TO LEARNING

21. **Achievement Motivation**—Young person is motivated to do well in school.

22. **School Engagement**—Young person is actively engaged in learning.

23. **Homework**—Young person reports doing at least one hour of homework every school day.

24. **Bonding to School**—Young person cares about her or his school.

25. **Reading for Pleasure**—Young person reads for pleasure three or more hours per week.

POSITIVE VALUES

26. **Caring**—Young person places high value on helping other people.

27. **Equality and Social Justice**—Young person places high value on promoting equality and reducing hunger and poverty.

28. **Integrity**—Young person acts on convictions and stands up for her or his beliefs.

29. **Honesty**—Young person "tells the truth even when it is not easy."

30. **Responsibility**—Young person accepts and takes personal responsibility.

31. **Restraint**—Young person believes it is important not to be sexually active or to use alcohol or other drugs.

SOCIAL COMPETENCIES

32. **Planning and Decision Making**—Young person knows how to plan ahead and make choices.

33. **Interpersonal Competence**—Young person has empathy, sensitivity, and friendship skills.

34. **Cultural Competence**—Young person has knowledge of and comfort with people of different cultural/racial/ethnic backgrounds.

35. **Resistance Skills**—Young person can resist negative peer pressure and dangerous situations.

36. **Peaceful Conflict Resolution**—Young person seeks to resolve conflict nonviolently.

POSITIVE IDENTITY

37. **Personal Power**—Young person feels he or she has control over "things that happen to me."

38. **Self-Esteem**—Young person reports having a high self-esteem.

39. **Sense of Purpose**—Young person reports that "my life has a purpose."

40. **Positive View of Personal Future**—Young person is optimistic about her or his personal future.

TOUGH
Experiences

ADDICTION

The prevalence of drug use, abuse, and addiction among teens is staggering. The *2006 Monitoring the Future* survey, which studies drug use in youth, revealed that 21 percent of students in grade 8, 36 percent of students in grade 10, and 48 percent of students in grade 12 have taken an illicit drug during their lifetime. Other highlights from this study: marijuana is by far the most widely used of the various illicit drugs; the use of LSD, other hallucinogens, powder cocaine, crystal methamphetamine, heroin, narcotics other than heroin, tranquilizers, club drugs (Ketamine, Rohypnol, GHB), and steroids shows no or very little decline from the previous year; and use of ecstasy, inhalants, and prescription drugs like OxyContin and Vicodin is increasing. The study also found that the prevalence of being drunk at least once in the prior month stands at 6 percent of students in grade 8, 19 percent of students in grade 10, and 30 percent of students in grade 12.[1]

In 2006, an estimated 22.6 million persons (9.2 percent of the population aged 12 or older) were classified with substance dependence or abuse in the past year, and 4 million persons aged 12 or older received some kind of treatment for a problem related to the use of alcohol or illicit drugs in 2006.[2]

It is important to differentiate between experimental chemical use, substance abuse, and addiction. Substance use is the experimental use of drugs and/or alcohol, which is often motivated by curiosity and is very short term, such as trying cigarettes once or twice. While experimentation is widespread, 90 percent of 12- to 17-year-olds choose to refrain from regular use.[3]

Substance abuse is the use of drugs or alcohol that leads to significant impairment or distress, and is demonstrated by things such as failure to fulfill major obligations at work, home, or school.[4]

Addiction is a chronic, relapsing condition characterized by compulsive drug seeking and abuse and by long-lasting chemical changes in the brain. Dependence on the addictive substance is at such a point that stopping is very difficult and causes several physical and mental reactions from withdrawal.[5] Addiction is recognized as a medical disorder, or disease, by many addiction specialists and therefore requires specialized treatment, as would any other disease. Only those with the appropriate professional licensure should diagnose and treat substance abuse and addiction.

Common Causes and Risk Factors for Chemical Use

A youth's environment and genetics will influence whether or not he will use, abuse, or become addicted to chemicals. Risk factors can increase a person's chances for drug abuse, while protective factors can reduce the risk. A risk factor for one person may not be a risk factor for another. The great news is, most individuals at risk for drug abuse do not start using drugs or become addicted.

Risk factors stem from the individual, family, school, friends, and community. Risk factors include addiction in the family, lack of parental supervision, substance abuse among peers, availability of drugs in the community, parental indifference about drug use, criminal behavior in the family, inconsistent parenting (such as unclear rules and boundaries), academic struggles, peer pressure, and antisocial behaviors (possibly psychiatric problems) in the youth or her family. The more risks a teen is exposed to, the more likely she will abuse drugs.[6]

We can work to counter these risks by providing youth with protective factors, such as prevention interventions. This could include interventions both in the family and at school that focus on helping youth develop appropriate, positive behaviors.

> "Speaking as a teen who was in and out of treatment centers, the only thing I have to say is, kids aren't going to quit drinking and using drugs just because adults want them to. It's unrealistic. Adults need to help teens think about the risks they're taking and recognize people have to make their own changes to quit using, and that may not be during adolescence."
> —Sam

WHAT YOU CAN DO TO HELP

Know the Warning Signs of Chemical Use and Abuse

People abuse many kinds of drugs, and each one comes with different warning signs of use. This section will provide a general overview of indications of chemical use and abuse. However, this is not an exhaustive list of warning signs, and these signs may indicate another problem entirely. Signs and symptoms of concern include:

Physical Signs

- Change in sleeping patterns; sleeping all the time; sleeping very little
- Dramatic weight loss/gain
- Bloodshot eyes, unusually large/small pupils, wearing sunglasses
- Runny nose
- Unusual smells (e.g., gasoline, tobacco)
- Thinning or loss of hair
- Bruises, skin abrasions
- Declining hygiene

Behavioral Signs

- Difficulty in school: truancy, declining grades, lack of interest in the future
- Lying, stealing, being manipulative
- Excessive irritability or happiness
- Excessive hunger
- Paranoia
- Lethargy, poor coordination, slurred speech, slowed breathing
- Sudden change in friends, secrecy about new friends
- Forgetfulness
- Depression, anxiety

If you are concerned, share your observations with the teen, and let her know someone is noticing changes. Contact a drug/alcohol specialist, share your specific concerns (without violating the confidentiality of the teen) and ask for recommendations.

Don't Wait for the Teen to Reach Out

It's a wonderful philosophy to wait patiently for people to share things when they're ready for us to know what is going on, but we shouldn't wait when we suspect chemical abuse/addiction. If you feel a teen is exhibiting warning signs, don't be afraid to reach out. All too often when we have concerns about kids, we share, or gossip, about our worries with other adults, but not directly with the youth about whom we're anxious. While we may need to share our concerns through proper supervision or collaboration, we should also direct our observations to the young person in question. Don't be afraid to reach out, and when you do, help teens verbalize what they need.

Be Realistic

Achieving absolute sobriety is an enormous goal for a chemically dependent teen. Rather than focusing on a lifelong goal of sobriety, focus on the here and now, which resonates more with teens. Talk about the consequences of chemical use and have teens be active participants in the conversation. For example, ask them about unprotected sex when using drugs and what the outcomes of this impaired decision could be. Ask them about their short-term goals: Do they want to graduate from high school? If they do, what are the ways using drugs will get in the way of this goal? Discuss the legal ramifications of drug/alcohol use: How could this behavior impact their goals?

Teens need to know we care about their safety and their future; some of the best prevention work we can do is in showing them we care.

Incorporate Harm Reduction

The central idea in harm reduction is that people will engage in behaviors that carry risks, such as drug use. Harm reduction's primary objective is to mitigate the potential dangers and health risks and reduce harm associated with or caused by drug use. Harm reduction does not support, condone, or excuse drug use; rather, it focuses on the health and safety of teens if they *do* use. Harm reduction may not be supported by your program or agency or personal philosophy, but it is a model worth learning more about. Harm reduction work with teens could include teaching them how to recognize

problem signs in themselves and others when using chemicals, and incorporating safety planning if they do use (e.g., identifying a designated driver). A resource for ideas on using the harm reduction approach with teens is the Drug Policy Alliance; see the following Resources section for contact information.

RESOURCES

Adolescent Substance Abuse Knowledge Base (adolescent-substance-abuse.com). Includes teen treatment directory, symptoms of specific drugs.

Drug Policy Alliance: Safety First Project (safety1st.org). A reality-based approach to teens and drugs. Includes downloadable fact sheets, downloadable resources for helpers.

National Adolescent Health Information Center (smmhp.psych.ucla.edu).

National Alcohol and Substance Abuse Information Center (addictioncareoptions.com). Phone: 800-784-6776.

National Institute on Drug Abuse (teens.drugabuse.gov). Includes links for parents and teachers, online quizzes for teens.

Recovery Resource Online (soberrecovery.com).

Substance Abuse Mental Health Services Administration (samhsa.gov). Phone: 800-662-HELP. A 24-hour substance abuse treatment helpline. Includes online self-tests to gauge your chemical abuse or someone else's, guides to action for communities, educators, and families, reproducible handouts on drugs, and ideas for prevention.

Addiction Proof Your Child: A Realistic Approach to Preventing Drug, Alcohol, and Other Dependencies by Stanton Peele. New York: Three Rivers Press, 2007.

NOTES

1. L. D. Johnson, P. M. O'Malley, J. G. Bachman, and J. E. Schulenberg, *Monitoring the Future: National Results on Adolescent Drug Use; Overview of Key Findings, 2006*, NIH Publication No. 07-6202 (Bethesda, MD: National Institute on Drug Abuse, 2007).

2. Substance Abuse and Mental Health Services Administration, *Results from the 2006 National Survey on Drug Use and Health: National Findings*, NSDUH Series H-32,

DHHS Publication No. SMA 07-4293, (Rockville, MD: Office of Applied Studies, 2007), www.oas.samhsa.gov/ p0000016.htm#2k6 (accessed September 27, 2007).

3. Substance Abuse and Mental Health Services Administration, *Results from the 2005 National Survey on Drug Use and Health: National Findings*, NSDUH Series H-30, DHHS Publication No. SMA 06-4194 (Rockville, MD: Office of Applied Studies, 2006), www.oas.samhsa.gov/p0000016 .htm#2k5 (accessed September 27, 2007).

4. American Psychiatric Association Staff, *Diagnostic and Statistical Manual of Mental Disorders*, 4th ed., text revision (Washington, DC: American Psychiatric Association, 2000.)

5. MedicineNet.com, "Definition of Addiction," www .medterms.com/script/main/art.asp?articlekey=10177 (accessed January 18, 2008).

6. National Institute on Drug Abuse, "Preventing Drug Abuse among Children and Adolescents," www.drugabuse .gov/Prevention/risk/html (accessed September 26, 2007).

Warning Signs of Chemical Use and Abuse

Physical Signs

- Change in sleeping patterns: sleeping all the time, sleeping very little

- Significant weight loss/gain

- Bloodshot eyes, unusually large/small pupils, wearing sunglasses, avoidance of eye contact

- Runny nose

- Unusual smells (e.g., gasoline, tobacco)

- Thinning or loss of hair

- Bruises, skin abrasions, rashes on face

- Declining hygiene and self-care

Behavioral Signs

- Difficulty in school: truancy, declining grades, lack of interest in the future

- Lying, stealing, being manipulative

- Excessive irritability or happiness

- Excessive hunger

- Paranoia

- Lethargy, poor coordination, slurred speech, slowed breathing

- Sudden change in friends, secrecy about new friends

- Forgetfulness

- Depression, anxiety

ANXIETY

Everyone feels worried and anxious at times—before a test, when in a new situation, or waiting to hear important news. These feelings of worry are normal and expected in certain situations. Problem anxiety is much more intense, pervasive, and not necessarily in reaction to a normal anxiety-provoking situation. Several types of anxiety disorders will be briefly described here: generalized anxiety disorder, social phobia, panic attacks, obsessive-compulsive disorder, and post-traumatic stress disorder.

TYPES OF ANXIETY DISORDERS

Generalized Anxiety Disorder

Generalized anxiety disorder is characterized by excessive anxiety and worrying for more than six months.[1] These worries are usually about many different things, such as school performance, performance in sports, or larger issues like natural disasters. A person with generalized anxiety disorder has difficulty controlling the worry, and she worries more days than not over a period of at least six months. A person with generalized anxiety disorder may feel restless, irritable, or tense. She may have difficulty falling or staying asleep, have problems concentrating, and may tire easily. Some people just naturally worry more than others, but when anxiety and worry become excessive and interfere with school, work, and social situations, it is time to consider the possibility of an anxiety disorder.

Social Phobia

The fundamental feature of social phobia (also known as social anxiety disorder) is a persistent fear and dread of social situations or performance situations because a person fears that he may be embarrassed in that situation. A person with this disorder has an intense fear of embarrassing himself in front of others and a dread of being seen in a negative light because of something he did. He is able to recognize that his fear is unreasonable and excessive, but feels helpless to control the fear. Common thoughts in someone who has social phobia may be "I'll do something embarrassing," or "People will think I'm stupid." Every teen has these thoughts from time to time, but someone with social phobia will go to great lengths to avoid situations where he could be embarrassed in public, and if such situations cannot be avoided, he will endure these situations with a great deal of anxiety and stress.[2]

Social phobia may be expressed as a general fear of most social situations, or it may be expressed in relationship to specific situations. The most common type of social phobia is stage fright, or performance anxiety. As with other types of anxiety disorders, social phobia can only be diagnosed when the avoidance, worrying while anticipating, and feelings during social situations begin to interfere with a person's school, work, and social life. The fear and avoidance may be so great that they totally disrupt a person's daily routine and activities. It is not considered social phobia when someone experiences fear and dread because he is under the influence of drugs.

Panic Attacks

A panic attack happens during a brief period of time and involves an overwhelming and sudden sense of fear, apprehension, or terror. During a panic attack, people often experience physical symptoms such as shortness of breath, shaking, chills or hot flashes, dizziness, heart palpitations, chest pain, choking sensations, or a fear of losing control.[3] Often people report that they feel as if they are having a heart attack, or are dying. During a panic attack, a person may feel an intense need to escape and usually has a sense of impending doom in the absence of any real danger. Having or even witnessing a panic attack can be frightening. Sometimes panic attacks occur unexpectedly and without any outside cue. Some people have panic attacks when they are in certain places or situations (for example, public speaking or driving). Panic attacks themselves are not a diagnosable mental illness, but they usually occur within the context of an anxiety disorder or other diagnosis.

"It got so bad I never wanted to leave my house. I was so afraid that I would be away from home and I would have a heart attack or die or do something really embarrassing. I will never forget driving along with my friend and thinking, 'I am dying.' I was crying and screaming and grabbing my heart and I couldn't breathe. I found out that was just a panic attack, but it felt so real! I was so scared to have another one and be embarrassed that I didn't want to hang out with my friends anymore." —Heather

Obsessive-Compulsive Disorder

Obsessive-compulsive disorder (often called OCD) is another type of anxiety disorder. The essential characteristics of OCD are recurrent obsessive thoughts and ritualistic behaviors that cause a person a significant amount of stress. Obsessions are intrusive and persistent thoughts, images, or impulses that may often repeat themselves. For example, a person may worry repeatedly that she has run over someone with her car. Someone with OCD realizes these thoughts are excessive and inappropriate, but feels unable to stop them. Compulsions are repetitive behaviors or mental acts that are often conducted in an effort to suppress or counteract the obsessions or thoughts. Examples of common compulsions are hand washing, double-checking for safety, or counting.[4]

Another example of OCD behavior is a person having obsessions (thoughts) about whether or not he left the stove on, and checking (compulsion) to see if it is still on. A third common example is a person who worries excessively about germs and washes his hands repeatedly. While it can be normal to see if you left the stove on, or to wash your hands if they feel dirty, a person with OCD would do such behaviors excessively (at least one hour per day), to the point where it would interfere with his daily routine. It is also possible to have only obsessive thoughts, without the corresponding compulsive behavior.

Post-Traumatic Stress Disorder

Post-Traumatic Stress Disorder (often called PTSD) is developed after experiencing or witnessing an extremely traumatic event. Such events include, but are not limited to, military combat, a physical assault, a sexual assault, being robbed or mugged, being kidnapped, natural disasters, car accidents, and being diagnosed with a terminal illness. You don't have to actually experience these events firsthand; you can be traumatized by hearing about a horrible event.

Symptoms of PTSD include recurrent and intrusive memories of the traumatic event and recurrent dreams of the event. Sometimes people will feel or act as though the event is happening again. People with PTSD might also feel a great amount of mental or physical distress when seeing or experiencing something that reminds them of the traumatic event. They will avoid situations, feelings, thoughts, and talking about things that may remind them of the traumatic event. They may also not be able to remember significant details about the traumatic event. Those with PTSD may feel detached from other people and have a restricted ability to show feelings. Symptoms of PTSD also include trouble sleeping, anger outbursts, concentration problems, and an exaggerated startle response (very jumpy and easily frightened).[5]

"It was like I saw him everywhere, even though I knew he was in jail. I was very jumpy and then I would think he was in the car next to me at the light or in the mall or wherever I was. I couldn't focus on school because I could only think of what he did. I even dreamed about it every night." —Sally

ABOUT ANXIETY DISORDERS

Why Do People Get Anxiety Disorders?

There are several factors that can put a person at risk for an anxiety disorder. The first of these are environmental factors. Young people without a strong support system, who live in violent environments, who live in poverty, or who have parents or caregivers who are anxious, are at a greater risk for developing anxiety disorders.[6] There are also hereditary and biological factors that can lead to anxiety.

People's personality traits may also leave them more at risk for an anxiety disorder; for example, people who worry a lot or those who feel they have very little control over their lives may be predisposed to anxiety disorders. Students who were rejected or neglected by their peers were found to have more social anxiety than popular or average students.[7] Experiencing a trauma is another factor that can lead to anxiety disorders—especially post-traumatic stress disorder.

Problems Associated with Untreated Anxiety

People with untreated anxiety disorders will not be able to live life to its full potential. Anxiety disorders can take over a person's life and disrupt school, work, and social relationships. Teens with anxiety disorders may have low self-esteem. They may lose or never make friends, fail in school, and have low attendance rates. They may act out in the classroom because anxiety is preventing them from sitting still and concentrating. Teens with untreated anxiety are also at risk for drug and alcohol use, sometimes as a means of self-medicating their symptoms. It is essential that someone with an anxiety disorder seek help.

WHAT YOU CAN DO TO HELP

If you suspect a teen has an anxiety disorder, you should immediately refer her or him to a doctor or therapist for treatment. However, *you* do not have to be a medical or mental health professional to help and support a young person with an anxiety disorder. Listening and communicating effectively is one of the best things you can do to help. Most people with anxiety disorders recognize that their fears are irrational and exaggerated. Reminding them of this fact is *not* helpful to them and may increase the amount of shame they have about the anxiety they are experiencing.

Be a calm presence with someone who is experiencing anxiety. Practice meditation and other relaxation techniques. Simple breathing and stretching exercises are easy ways of bringing about calmer feelings. Once you learn how these techniques work, you can share them with teens who are distressed. Yoga and tai chi can also be very effective in reducing anxiety and stress.

"I have such physical symptoms from my anxiety, like heartburn. I just have constant, constant fear and try not to show it. I wish someone could teach me how to cope with it, because I just drink and watch TV to deal with it. I also think if the things I am good at, like art, was more socially valued, I would feel less anxious." —Michael

Set a good example of pro-social behavior. Invite a teen to new, nonstressful social situations. If she is very anxious, socialize at first only with people she knows and is comfortable with. Enjoy a volunteer opportunity together. Ask about the teen's hobbies and interests and try to participate in these activities with her.

Encouraging healthy physical and dietary habits is one easy way of supporting someone with an anxiety disorder. Take it a step further and offer to go for a walk or participate in some other physical exercise. Offer healthy snacks and stay away from junk food when you are with a teen who is dealing with anxiety. Encourage healthy sleep habits as well: being overtired can make anxiety worse. Avoiding caffeine and other stimulants is important, since these substances can exacerbate anxiety symptoms.

RESOURCES

American Counseling Association (counseling.org). The official Web site of the American Counseling Association. Resources and information on where to find a counselor are provided.

Anxiety Disorders Association of America (adaa.org). Information from a nonprofit organization dedicated to education about anxiety disorders.

HealthyPlace.com—Anxiety Community (healthyplace .com). Information about relaxation techniques.

Mental Health America (www1.nmha.org). Basic information and definitions of anxiety and anxiety disorders.

National Alliance on Mental Illness (nami.org). Grassroots organization that aims to improve the lives of people with mental illness.

If Your Adolescent Has an Anxiety Disorder: An Essential Resource for Parents (Adolescent Mental Health Initiative) by Edna Foa and Linda Wasmer Andrews. New York: Oxford University Press, 2006.

Living Fully with Shyness and Social Anxiety: A Comprehensive Guide to Gaining Social Confidence by Erika Hilliard. New York: Marlowe and Company, 2005.

NOTES

1. American Psychiatric Association Staff, *Diagnostic and Statistical Manual of Mental Disorders*, 4th ed., text revision (Washington, DC: American Psychiatric Association, 2000).

2. Ibid.

3. Ibid.

4. Ibid.

5. Ibid.

6. Helpguide, www.helpguide.org/mental/anxiety_types_symptoms_treatment.htm (accessed September 12, 2007).

7. H. M. Inderbitzen, K. S. Walters, and A. L. Bukowski, "The Role of Social Anxiety in Adolescent Peer Relations: Differences among Sociometric Status Groups and Rejected Subgroups," *Journal of Clinical Child Psychology* 26 (1997): 338–348.

What Can You Do
If You Have an Anxiety Disorder?

The most important thing to do if you think you have an anxiety disorder is to tell an adult you trust about your feelings. See if he or she can help you get an appointment with a doctor, counselor, or other health professional. You should also know that there are millions of people with anxiety disorders, so you are not crazy or alone!

In addition to getting professional help, there are several small things you can do to help ease your anxiety. Exercise, eating well, and good sleep are all important to good mental health. Anxiety can get worse if you drink too much caffeine, eat foods that are bad for you, and become overtired. Exercise can be as simple as walking or riding a bike. Some people with anxiety have stomach problems, so staying away from greasy foods can help ease some of these symptoms. Sometimes people with anxiety have trouble falling asleep or staying asleep; allowing yourself enough time to sleep and getting in the habit of allowing time to sleep can help you feel less tired and more able to deal with your anxiety.

Participating in meditation, relaxation techniques, yoga, or tai chi can increase your ability to calm yourself. Simple breathing exercises and relaxation techniques can also help reduce stress. Being with friends you feel comfortable around is also a good way to relieve stress. Creating a list of people (friends and adults) who can support you is a great way to be prepared when feeling anxious. You can look at the list and make calls to or plans with people who understand you and your anxiety. Remember, you are not the only person who feels anxious, and there are people in your life who would like to help you feel better.

And if the suggestions here do not seem to help you, don't let that make you even *more* anxious. One of the biggest signs of an anxiety disorder is the fact that regular calming techniques don't always work. Discuss your difficulties with a counselor or doctor.

Simple and Easy Relaxation Techniques

Breathe: Doing intentional, deep breathing is one way to relax and ease stress.

- Close your eyes (if you are comfortable doing so).
- Breathe in through your nose for 5 to 7 seconds—pay attention to the breaths and make sure your stomach is going out while you do this.
- Breathe out through your mouth for 7 to 10 seconds.
- Repeat this 5 times.

Progressive relaxation: This is an exercise in tightening and relaxing your muscles from your toes to your head.

- Lie down, or sit comfortably in a chair with your feet on the floor and your arms resting at your sides.
- Close your eyes (if you are comfortable doing so).
- Starting with your toes, squeeze your muscles, and hold for 5 to 10 seconds. Release the tension and repeat 2 more times.
- Next, move up to your calves and squeeze and release them. Do this 3 times.
- Repeat this sequence moving up your body: thighs, buttocks, hands, stomach, shoulders, and finally your face.
- Once you have repeated the entire sequence for your whole body, rest and enjoy the relaxed feelings.
- This is also a great way to fall asleep if you are having trouble doing so.

Take a warm bath or shower: Relaxing in the tub is a great way to ease your body and your mind.

Listen to calming music: Pay attention to the music as it plays—this can help you focus and clear your mind.

Laugh: Laughing is a great way to break tension. Watch a funny movie or TV show.

Take a walk: Walking around the block or even just walking away from a stressful situation for a few minutes will calm your nerves.

Try tai chi or yoga: Take a class, or check out a DVD from the public library. Both of these types of exercise can help you focus and center yourself.

Reprinted with permission from *Helping Teens Handle Tough Experiences: Strategies to Foster Resilience*, by Jill Nelson and Sarah Kjos. Copyright © 2008 by Search Institute®, Minneapolis, Minnesota, 800-888-7828, www.search-institute.org. All rights reserved.

ATTENTION AND BEHAVIOR DISORDERS

This chapter focuses on attention deficit hyperactivity disorder (ADHD) and oppositional defiant disorder (ODD). The two disorders are discussed together here because they may be confused with each other at times—indeed, they appear under the same classification in the American Psychiatric Association's Diagnostic and Statistical Manual of Mental Disorders. The information here is intended to help readers distinguish between the two.

ATTENTION DEFICIT HYPERACTIVITY DISORDER

The fundamental features of ADHD are chronic inattentiveness and/or hyperactivity or impulsivity that is more severe compared to that of other people at the same age and stage of development.[1] ADHD is classified one of three ways: inattentive type, hyperactive-impulsive type, or combined type.

Behaviors and attitudes that are typical of *inattention* include failure to pay attention to details in schoolwork or work, difficulties paying attention while doing tasks and play, and not paying attention when being spoken to. Inattentive behaviors also include not following through with instructions, failing to finish tasks, and difficulties with organizing tasks. Teens with ADHD may have no interest in doing homework or other tasks that require a lot of attention, may forget about everyday things, and may be easily distracted by outside stimuli (for example, a noise in the hallway or another student shuffling papers).[2]

Behaviors that can be described as *hyperactive* include fidgeting or squirming in place or leaving a chair when it is time to sit, and talking excessively. A child with hyperactive behaviors may climb or run around excessively and act as if she is driven by a motor; in adolescents and adults the outward behaviors may not be there, but they may experience feelings of restlessness.[3] *Impulsive* behaviors include difficulties waiting turns, blurting out answers out of turn or before questions have even been finished, and interrupting or butting in on others' conversations or activities.

Who Has ADHD?

It is estimated that 3 to 7 percent of school-age youth have ADHD.[4] Sometimes symptoms of ADHD are most visible in childhood and gradually lessen in adolescence and adulthood. ADHD seems to run in families, but any youth is at risk for developing ADHD. School factors, social factors, and family support all play a role in the extent to which ADHD negatively affects a person. A supportive environment can go a long way toward helping someone with ADHD succeed.

Diagnosing ADHD

It can be difficult to diagnose ADHD, and it is often misdiagnosed. Children at different developmental stages exhibit different levels of activity, and it's important to consider their stages of development and weigh their behaviors against those of other children of the same age to get an idea of whether the inattentive, hyperactive, or impulsive behaviors are more severe than in other children of the same age. In order to obtain a medical diagnosis for ADHD, these symptoms must be present and cause difficulties in more than one setting, such as school, work, or home.

There is no medical test for ADHD, but a physician will likely do a medical examination to rule out other physical disorders that may have similar symptoms. Only trained professionals—physicians, psychologists, and licensed social workers or counselors—can give a diagnosis of ADHD. The process of getting a diagnosis of ADHD requires input from several people in the youth's life, including parents or caregivers and teachers. There will be questions and discussions about inattentive, hyperactive, and impulsive behaviors. Parents, caregivers, and teachers may be asked to complete a checklist of symptoms. A large number of people diagnosed with ADHD may also have other mental health diagnoses, so an accurate and professional diagnosis is essential for providing the best treatment and interventions for someone with ADHD.

Positives about ADHD

Not everything about ADHD is bad. People with ADHD are sometimes stereotyped as running around like crazy and unable to control their own behaviors. This is far from the truth. People with ADHD are often vibrant and creative. They tend to be flexible and open to change.

WHAT YOU CAN DO TO HELP

Recommend an Evaluation

If you suspect a teen has undiagnosed ADHD, it is important to encourage the teen to get a medical evaluation (be sure to involve the parents or guardians as required), because there are several medical conditions with symptoms that mimic those

of ADHD, including lead poisoning, side effects of some medications such as those used to treat asthma, and thyroid problems.[5] A common but sometimes controversial way of treating ADHD is with medication. Even if medication is prescribed, most people with ADHD benefit a great deal from counseling or behavioral coaching. Even if you are not a medical or counseling professional there are many things you can do to support a teen with ADHD.

> "People who actually have ADHD are less likely to admit they have it because it's like you're admitting you're stupid. ADHD is referred to so much in a joking way, 'Oh, I have ADD!' and that takes away from the significance of how difficult it really is to live with ADHD. It's not easy to have 600 things happening in your head at once, it's hard to filter through all that. I had a lot of shame about the way I functioned as a teen with ADHD, I was really sensitive to any innuendo about me needing to be quiet— I didn't have a lot of control about me talking about 25 things at once. Maybe my ADHD has been a gift, I get to absorb so much around me that maybe others can't." —Lori

Be ADHD-Friendly

If you are a parent, teacher, or someone who works with teens with ADHD, you can set up an environment that is ADHD-friendly. First, relay your expectations in a clear and concise manner. If a teen understands what is expected, it will be easier for her to comply. After you have given directions or explained your expectations, check to see if your message was heard. If you are planning activities or lesson plans, allow time for things other than sitting and listening (which can be very difficult for a teen with ADHD). Allow time for "stretch breaks" and hands-on activities.

If you are working with a teen who has symptoms of inattention, it is important to help him maintain focus by lessening distractions. People who do not have ADHD have fewer problems focusing on what is important; a person with ADHD can focus, but often he will focus on too many things at once. Turning off the TV, having conversations with others in a different room, and being in a space with few posters, open windows, or other visual elements are all easy ways of limiting distractions in the environment.

If the teen you are working with has symptoms of hyperactivity and impulsivity, bear in mind that sitting for long periods of time will be difficult for her. Also remember that while she is sitting down, she may fidget, squirm in her seat, or tap her foot rapidly. If these behaviors are not interfering with other people, it is best not to reprimand her for doing them. Teens with impulsivity may interrupt others and be quick to answer questions you haven't finished asking. Being patient and giving feedback about the appropriateness of this behavior can help them understand how their behavior affects others. Teens with ADHD are not usually fidgeting or interrupting to be rude: it is a symptom of their illness. Gently prompting and guiding their behavior to more appropriate channels will help them gain insight into their behaviors.

It is also vital to praise teens with ADHD for what they do well. Teens with ADHD are likely to feel frustrated with school and question their abilities. People with ADHD can be very creative, energetic, and fun; let them know about the good things you see, not just the frustrating things.

OPPOSITIONAL DEFIANT DISORDER

The elemental feature of oppositional defiant disorder (ODD) is a pattern of negative, disobedient, and defiant behaviors toward authority figures.[6] In order to get a diagnosis of ODD, these behaviors need to be present for at least six months. The behaviors associated with ODD usually start at home, gradually worsen in severity, and spread into other venues (school and work) over time. Instances of negativity and defiance are natural in a teen's development; it is when the symptoms are substantially worse than the behaviors of a teen's peers that ODD can be diagnosed.

Symptoms of ODD

Some of the negative and disobedient behaviors include having a short temper, being argumentative with adults, deliberately annoying others, and refusing to do what is asked or refusing to follow rules. Someone with ODD may blame others for her mistakes, be easily annoyed by others, be very angry, or be spiteful and vindictive. Again, many of these behaviors sound like "normal" teenage behavior; a diagnosis is made when these behaviors are severe enough to cause trouble at school, work, in social settings, or at home, are consistent, and last more than six months.

Who Has ODD?

It is estimated that between 30 and 40 percent (and possibly as many as 60 to 65 percent) of all children with ADHD may also have oppositional defiant disorder.[7] There is often a spiral effect of worsening behaviors when dealing with a teen with ODD. By the time a teen with ODD reaches adolescence, he may have a history of school behavior problems that lead to social and academic problems. He may have alienated many of the adults and more positive peers in his life. These factors can lead to lowered self-esteem, which in turn can increase the number of or intensity of his oppositional behaviors. It can be very frustrating to parent, teach, or work with someone with ODD, but there are things you can do to help a teen develop more positive behaviors.

WHAT YOU CAN DO TO HELP

Connect with Professional Resources

If you suspect that a teen has ODD, it is important to connect him and his family or caregivers with professional help, which includes a medical evaluation and counseling. Oppositional defiant disorder frequently coexists with other mental health problems, such as ADHD, depression, and anxiety. While medication is not usually prescribed for ODD alone, medication is sometimes appropriate for the coexisting disorder.

Individual outpatient counseling for the teen is recommended, especially in the earlier and milder stages of ODD. Many teens who end up in a group home or inpatient environment have a diagnosis of ODD. Sometimes the behaviors associated with ODD (especially noncompliance with rules) can eventually lead to legal problems and possible probation. Intervening early can hopefully decrease the likelihood of legal troubles or court-remanded counseling. Counseling for the teen may focus on new ways of dealing with anger, working on emotional regulation, and gaining insight into her oppositional behaviors. She may learn social skills and appropriate ways of addressing her feelings. Family counseling can help the teen and caregiver work together and provide outside support to a family that may very well be struggling. Another way professionals can help is by educating and supporting the adults who are raising a young person with ODD.

RESOURCES

American Academy of Child and Adolescent Psychiatry (aacap.org).

Children and Adults with Attention Deficit / Hyperactivity Disorder (chadd.org). An organization dedicated to improving the lives of people affected by ADHD and ADD.

MisUnderstood Minds from PBS (pbs.org). Interactive activities that mimic ADHD.

ADHD: Attention-Deficit Hyperactivity Disorder in Children and Adults by P. H. Wender. London: Oxford University Press, 2002.

Attention Deficit Disorder: A Different Perception by Thom Hartmann. Grass Valley, CA: Underwood Books, 1997.

The Edison Gene: ADHD and the Gift of the Hunter Child by Thom Hartmann. Rochester, VT: Park Street Press, 2003.

Taking Charge of ADHD by R. A. Barkley. New York: The Guilford Press, 2000.

NOTES

1. American Psychiatric Association Staff, *Diagnostic and Statistical Manual of Mental Disorders*, 4th ed., text revision (Washington, DC: American Psychiatric Association, 2000).

2. Ibid.

3. Ibid.

4. Ibid.

5. Ibid.

6. Ibid.

7. M. Kuhne and R. Schachar, "Impact of Comorbid Oppositional or Conduct Problems on Attention-Deficit Hyperactivity Disorder," *Journal of the American Academy of Child and Adolescent Psychiatry* 36 (1997): 1715–1725.

Things Teens with ADHD
Can Do to Help Themselves

If you know you have ADHD, or if you find yourself having a hard time concentrating, there are several things you can do to help yourself. These helpful tips are adapted from kidshealth.org:

Sit at the front of the class, or away from friends you are tempted to talk to.

Tell your teachers or other adults you work with about your ADHD—they can be more helpful if they know.

Tell your friends about your ADHD. Keeping your friends informed about ADHD may help them understand you better.

Stay organized. Keep a homework journal and schedule your time each day.

Exercise. Take breaks to do physical activities during school breaks and while doing homework.

Practice relaxation techniques or learn meditation.

Remember the things you do well: give yourself credit and don't get too down on yourself.

Dealing with Teens
Who Have Oppositional Defiant Disorder

Choose your battles. Teens with oppositional defiant disorder may want to break rules and engage in power struggles. Determine the things you are not willing to compromise on and set clear limits regarding them.

See the positives. What is he doing well? What are his positive qualities? Look for positives and praise the teen for those things. Someone with ODD gets a lot of feedback about what he does wrong—let him know when you appreciate the positive too!

If you are getting frustrated or angry, take a break or a time-out. Let the teen know you need a minute or two before you can finish the discussion, and walk away from the situation for a moment. Not only will you avoid blowing up or saying something you regret, but you also model a good anger management skill.

Take care of yourself. A teen with ODD can be overwhelming to deal with at times. Schedule adult time away from the youth you work with so you can renew your energy.

BULLYING AND RELATIONAL AGGRESSION

Every year, millions of children and teens encounter bullying behavior. Bullying can be described as aggressive acts of physical, emotional, or social violence that are used to wield power over or cause distress to another person, and deliberately harm that person. The bully, or aggressor, holds power over the victim, and the bullying behavior is unprovoked. Typically, and for the purposes of this chapter, "bullying" refers to physical acts, and "relational aggression" will refer to acts of emotional and social violence.

Bullying behaviors include pushing, shoving, hitting, tripping, and destroying property. Relational aggression behaviors include name-calling, gossip, rumor spreading, teasing, picking on someone's appearance, ignoring or excluding, sarcastic comments, racial or ethnic slurs, and verbal abuse. Boys are more likely to support or be involved in bullying behavior, and girls are more likely to participate in relational aggression.

Sometimes people see bullying behaviors or relational aggression in action and chalk it up to typical kid or teen behavior. While these behaviors may unfortunately be common, they are not "typical," and they can be extremely harmful to everyone involved.

Consequences of Bullying and Relational Aggression

Bullying is the most prevalent form of aggression in schools.[1] Bullying interferes with learning and can cause an increase in school absences and dropouts. Other consequences of bullying include students feeling less safe and satisfied with school, a loss of self-esteem, and a higher risk for depression.

Bullying can have long-term effects for perpetrators as well. Children who are bullies may become adult bullies and are more likely to abuse children and their partners. Children who are identified as bullies by the age of eight are six times more likely to have a criminal conviction by the age of 24.[2]

Identifying Victims of Bullying and Relational Aggression

Sometimes bullying is easy to identify—for instance, when you witness someone pushing or shoving another student. But more often, bullying is covert. Teens who use relational aggression against other teens are often "just" using words, and can easily deny that they said anything hurtful, especially if an adult didn't hear what was said. Further, teens may not always tell adults what is going on at school.

Certain signs and symptoms may be associated with someone who is a victim of bullying or relational aggression. Victims may show emotional signs such as sadness, feelings of rejection, withdrawal from others, and mood swings.[3] Someone who is being bullied may not want to go to school, or may start skipping school. Books and other possessions may be broken or damaged, or go missing. Someone who is being bullied may walk without confidence and avoid eye contact with others. A particularly dangerous sign that someone is being bullied is that he begins to threaten violence to himself or others; he may even want to bring weapons to school. Long-term bullying and relational aggression can result in depression and other mental illnesses, and can even lead to suicide.[4] If you have serious concerns about the mental health of a student who is being bullied, it is wise to seek professional help from a counselor or other mental health professional. Often, developing a trusting relationship with a teen and talking to him is the only way to know if he is being bullied.

Identifying Bullies and Relationally Aggressive Teens

Bullies may seem to dominate others and thrive on being the most powerful person in a group. A bully may seem to enjoy making others feel bad and have little remorse about causing others pain or discomfort. Bullies may have a history of aggressive behaviors; they may have discipline problems or difficulties controlling their anger.[5] Girls who are relationally aggressive may believe that it is acceptable to start rumors about someone, or may have little awareness about what is considered socially aggressive or mean.[6] Because bullying behavior typically begins in childhood, teens who bully may be very good at hiding their bullying behaviors from adults. If you suspect you are parenting or working with a teen who is a bully, it is important that you relay the message that bullying is not acceptable.

WHAT YOU CAN DO TO HELP

Preventing Bullying and Relational Aggression

One way to prevent bullying is to help keep a young person from becoming a victim. Teens who have self-confidence and good social skills, and who are willing to seek help from trusted adults, are less likely to become victims of bullying and relational aggression. Modeling nonviolence, respect, and positive conflict management skills will assist in preventing children from becoming bullies.[7] Helping children and teens on an individual basis is one way of preventing or stopping bullying and relational aggression. As an adult working with teens, it is vital that you send a clear message that bullying will not be tolerated. You can also work to increase teens' conflict resolution skills and social skills.[8]

Make Systemic Changes

Bullying and relational aggression are often schoolwide problems that require intervention at a systemwide level. Several excellent bullying education and prevention programs are available for purchase, and many of them have been shown to reduce the rate of bullying and relational aggression. Typically these programs involve educating students, parents, teachers and other stakeholders about bullying and relational aggression. They also include a means of assessing the level of the bullying problem and offer an intervention program that can be implemented. The intervention program may include ways to teach students, teachers, and parents how to confront bullying and reward nonbullying, prosocial behavior. Bullying prevention programs will also include ways to measure and assess bullying behavior after the program has been implemented, so users can know if the prevention program was successful at reducing bullying and relational aggression. Each organization must choose a bullying prevention program that suits its needs.

Bullying is a social problem that causes harm to everyone involved—from childhood into adulthood. Preventing bullying early and confronting bullying behaviors is important to teens' success.

RESOURCES

Bullying.org (bullying.org). An organization dedicated to eliminating bullying, with several resources for kids and adults.

Conflict Resolution Network (crnhq.org).

Cyberbullying.org (cyberbullying.org). Maintained by the creator of bullying.org, this site focuses specifically on the issue of bullying in cyberspace.

Stop Bullying Now! (stopbullyingnow.hrsa.gov). Contains many free resources for children and adults.

And Words Can Hurt Forever: How to Protect Adolescents from Bullying, Harassment, and Emotional Violence by James Garbarino and Ellen deLara. New York: Free Press, 2002.

Girl Wars: 12 Strategies That Will End Female Bullying by Cheryl Dellasega and Charisse Nixon. New York: Simon & Schuster, 2003.

Odd Girl Out: The Hidden Culture of Aggression in Girls by Rachel Simmons. New York: Harcourt, 2002.

Reviving Ophelia: Saving the Selves of Adolescent Girls by Mary Pipher. New York: Putnam, 1994.

NOTES

1. M. B. Greene, "Bullying in Schools: A Plea for Measure of Human Rights," *Journal of Social Issues* 62 (2006): 63–79.

2. U.S. Department of Health and Human Services: Substance Abuse and Mental Health Services Administration (SAMHSA), *Taking Action Against Bullying*, 2003, download.ncadi.samhsa.gov/ken/pdf/SVP-0056/SVP-0056 .pdf (accessed October 25, 2007).

3. Ibid.

4. Dellasega and Nixon, *Girl Wars: 12 Strategies That Will End Female Bullying* (New York: Simon & Schuster, 2003).

5. U.S. Department of Health and Human Services, *Taking Action Against Bullying*.

6. Dellasega and Nixon, *Girl Wars*.

7. U.S. Department of Health and Human Services, *Taking Action Against Bullying*.

8. N. Mullin-Rindler, "New Fixes for Relational Aggression," *Education Digest* 69 (2003): 9–11.

Signs and Symptoms Displayed by Victims of Bullies

- Experience sadness and feelings of rejection
- Withdraw from others
- Have mood swings
- Avoid school or after-school activities
- Display lack of self-esteem
- "Lose" money or have possessions that are inexplicably damaged or missing
- Avoid eye contact
- Have unexplained injuries
- Threat violence to self or others

Signs and Symptoms Displayed by Bullies

- Dominate others
- Thrive on being the most powerful person in a group
- Seem to enjoy making others feel bad
- Show little remorse about causing others pain or discomfort
- Have little awareness about what is considered socially aggressive or mean
- Have a history of aggressive behavior
- Have difficulty controlling anger

How to Respond to Bullying

Create a bully-free culture. Make a bully-free culture a priority for your school, program, or agency.

Be mindful of your surroundings. Pay attention to the interactions between teens and support those who may bullied.

Confront the behavior. Let the bully know that such behaviors are not acceptable.

- Identify for the bully the specific behaviors that you observed and explain that such behaviors aren't acceptable.

- Don't get into an argument or power struggle about whether or not the bully was intending to target the victim.

CHEMICALLY DEPENDENT PARENTS OR CAREGIVERS

The chapter on addiction (page 15) discusses addiction and chemical dependence in relation to teens, but much of that information also applies to adults—particularly in terms of the behavioral differences between experimentation, addiction, and dependence, and the risk factors that can lead someone to become chemically dependent. Teens who have chemically dependent parents or caregivers can experience the secondary effects of addiction: instability in the home, difficulty in school, and trouble forming positive relationships with peers and adults.

According to the most recent study available, there were an estimated 28.6 million children of alcoholics in the United States in 1991, nearly 11 million of them under age 18. Of the under-18 group, almost 3 million will develop alcoholism, other drug problems, and/or other serious coping problems.[1] Teens may have biological parents who are addicts (either using or in recovery) and/or caregivers (such as foster parents or grandparents) who are addicts. Whether or not the teen lives with the caregiver who is addicted, she can be affected by the adult's addiction.

Parental substance abuse can have emotional, behavioral, medical, and educational consequences on teens. Because parents who abuse alcohol or drugs are more likely to experience domestic violence, divorce, unemployment, mental illness, and legal problems, their ability to parent effectively is severely compromised. There is a higher prevalence of the following issues in teens who have addicted parents: depression, anxiety, eating disorders, suicide attempts, their own addictions, physical and sexual abuse, lower self-esteem, witnessing violence, difficulty focusing in school due to tensions at home, economic difficulties, stress-related health problems, absenteeism, taking on developmentally inappropriate responsibility for household/family members, and lack of adequate supervision.[2]

> "It was scary, just scary when my dad would drink. Sometimes he would get in accidents, sometimes he would hurt my mom. It was easier just to pretend nothing was wrong."
> —Hannah

WHAT YOU CAN DO TO HELP

Understand the Emotional Impact

Adolescents who grow up with an addicted parent may experience an emotional reality unlike that of a youth who grows up without addicted parents. By being aware of the common feelings of children of addicts, we are better equipped to help teens explore these emotions and make appropriate referrals. These emotional impacts include:

Guilt: Teen may start to believe he is responsible for his loved one's drug use; he may become afraid to talk about the problems at home.

Anxiety: Teen may worry constantly about the situation at home. May fear the addicted parent will become sick or injured; may also fear fights and violence between parents.

Embarrassment: Parents may give their children the message that there is a terrible secret at home. The ashamed teen does not invite friends home and is afraid to ask anyone for help.

Inability to have close relationships: Because the using parent has disappointed the teen many times, she does not trust others.

Anger: Teen feels anger at the addicted parent for using, may feel he would be better off without the guardian who uses. He may be angry or lose respect for a nonaddicted parent for lack of support and protection.

Confusion: Teen may have conflicted feelings toward person who is addicted (love her, hate the behaviors).

Fear: Teen may live in fear of the unpredictable behaviors and circumstances of home. She may worry that the parent who is addicted will embarrass her or damage her relationships with peers, teachers, and others.

Depression: Teen feels lonely and helpless to change the situation.[3]

Convey Hope

It is critical to have hope for each youth and not assume that because he is raised by an addict he is "doomed." Yes, he is at greater risk for more behavioral, emotional, and medical consequences than his peers raised by nonaddicted parents, but it does not mean he cannot be resistant to the addiction. Foster this resilience through support for the teen, encouraging healthy choices, teaching coping skills, and offering community-based activities and programs that provide safe havens for teens. Kids raised by addicts need our optimism and hope; ask yourself how you can convey hope to a youth you are concerned for and put these ideas into action.

Be a Stabilizing Influence

Developing trust in an adult is important for all teens, and may be more difficult for teens living with addiction in the family. Teens need a stable and consistent adult whom they trust. Just by being a stable and consistent person in a teen's life, you are providing her the opportunity to trust. Respect your relationship and the teen's disclosures by sharing her story with others only when professionally necessary. Be a stable influence by not making empty promises. While it may be our mission to make things better for teens, we cannot guarantee we can do this, and should not tell teens this is something we can do.

Although being a stable, consistent, and positive adult in a youth's life can feel like it lacks impact in the here and now, it's one of the best things we can do to help teens cope with difficult experiences. Show teens you are a reliable (and predictable) adult both in your consistent care and structure, and by creating traditions with the teens with whom you work.

Reinforce "It's Not Your Fault"

Addiction is a disease, and you should share with teens, in a developmentally appropriate manner, the hows and whys of addiction. Remind teens they are not the reason their guardians abuse chemicals, and because they are not the reason, they cannot stop it. This message should be sent as often as a teen exhibits guilt for a guardian's chemical dependency. Refrain from any statements that imply a youth would ever be responsible for an adult's chemical dependency.

Keep It Simple: Listen

When a youth describes how someone or something is making him hurt, it's hard not to criticize the source of the pain. No matter how we feel, it serves no beneficial purpose to berate a teen's parent(s). Focus on the teen and his thoughts and feelings; if you need to vent, share your frustrations about the addicted person with co-workers, not the teen. Provide teens with opportunities and experiences to let out their emotions—through conversation, art, or whatever reaches them. If you have the ability to connect with the parent who is addicted, encourage chemical dependency treatment and make appropriate referrals.

Have Literature on Hand

Create a list of referrals for treatment and professional help for teens and adults. Gather brochures and handouts on addiction and chemical abuse in the family and have them readily available. You can contact the agencies listed in the Resources portion of this chapter to order free material. Resources may also be available through your public health department and state department of human services. Giving kids information that mirrors their life experiences can help normalize their thoughts and emotions and help with feelings of isolation or loneliness.

RESOURCES

Al-Anon Family Group Headquarters, Inc. (al-anon.org). Phone: 888-4AL-ANON

Alateen, for teenagers living in an alcoholic home (alateen.org)

Children of Alcoholics Foundation (coaf.org). Phone: 212-595-5810 ext. 7760

Families Anonymous (familiesanonymous.org). Groups for concerned relatives and friends whose lives have been adversely affected by a loved one's addiction. Includes meeting directory.

Join Together (jointogether.org). Works to advance effective alcohol and drug policy, prevention, and treatment. Includes specific ideas for community action based on your roles/career.

National Association for Children of Alcoholics (nacoa.org). Site includes downloadable kit for educators, info for teens, prevention handbook for clergy, and social-work curriculum materials.

NOTES

1. Substance Abuse and Mental Health Services Administration, "The Fact Is . . . Alcoholism Tends to Run in Families," 1995, Publication No. ADM 92-1914, ncadi.samhsa.gov/govpubs/ph318 (accessed September 30, 2007).

2. Children of Alcoholics Foundation, "Effects of Parental Substance Abuse on Children and Families," www.coaf .org/professionals/effects%20.htm (accessed September 30, 2007).

3. American Academy of Child and Adolescent Psychiatry, "Facts for Families: Children of Alcoholics," 2002, aacap.org/page.ww?name=Children+of+Alcholics &section=Facts+for+Families (accessed September 30, 2007).

Helping Teens Who Have
Chemically Dependent Parents or Caregivers

Understand the emotional impact. Adolescents who grow up with an addicted parent may experience guilt, anxiety, embarrassment, anger, confusion, fear, depression, and an inability to have close relationships. By being aware of these common feelings, we can be better equipped to help teens explore these emotions and make appropriate referrals.

Be aware of other consequences. Parental substance abuse can have behavioral, medical, and educational consequences on teens. They experience a higher incidence of depression, difficulty in school, low self-esteem, absenteeism, anxiety, and their own addictions.

Convey hope. It is critical that the youth not assume that because he is raised by an addict he is "doomed." Foster his resilience through support for the teen, encouraging healthy choices, teaching coping skills, and making him aware of community-based activities and programs that provide safe havens.

Be a stabilizing influence. Teens need a stable and consistent adult whom they trust. Just by being a stable and consistent person in a teen's life, you are providing her the opportunity to trust.

Reinforce "It's not your fault." Addiction is a disease. Remind teens that they are not the reason their guardians abuse chemicals, and because they are not the reason, they cannot stop it.

Don't criticize the parents. No matter how we feel, it serves no beneficial purpose to berate a teen's parent(s). Focus on the teen and his thoughts and feelings; if you need to vent, share your frustrations about the addicted person with co-workers, not the teen.

Have literature on hand. Create a list of referrals for treatment and professional help for teens and adults.

DATING VIOLENCE

Dating violence is the use of physical, sexual, emotional, and/or verbal abuse to exert power and control over the victim. Like all forms of violence, it is a choice made by the abuser. Dating violence occurs in heterosexual and homosexual relationships and in short-term and longer relationships. As with other forms of abuse, anyone can become a victim. Examples of ways one partner can control the other include pinching, grabbing, intimidating, forced sexual contact, threats, insults, accusations of cheating, isolating the partner from friends and family, and failing to take responsibility for the abusive behaviors. Like domestic violence, the abuse often becomes more severe as the relationship continues.

Liz Claiborne Inc. commissioned Teenage Research Unlimited to conduct a survey to reach a deeper understanding of the prevalence of teen dating violence. Their astounding 2006 results include:

- 1 in 2 teens who have been in a serious relationship say they've gone against their beliefs in order to please their partner.

- 1 in 3 girls who have been in a serious relationship say they've been concerned about being physically hurt by their partner.

- 23 percent of girls who have been in a relationship reported going further sexually than they wanted as a result of pressure from their partner.

- 1 in 5 teens who have been in a serious relationship report being hit, slapped, or pushed by a partner.

- 61 percent of teens said that they've had a boyfriend or girlfriend who made them feel bad or embarrassed about themselves.

- 1 in 4 teens who have been in a serious relationship say their boyfriend or girlfriend has tried to prevent them from spending time with friends or family; the same number have been pressured to only spend time with their partner.[1]

"I didn't even know I was in an abusive relationship while it was going on, I just knew something was really wrong. I never heard girls talking about their boyfriends hurting them or scaring them, so I felt like such an outsider. I never heard adults talking about dating violence. I didn't know what to do with what was going on but keep it a secret." —Leia

41

The prevalence of teen dating violence cannot be ignored and is just as serious as other forms of violence. This chapter will generally speak of victims as female, since a higher percentage of victims of dating violence are female, but males can also be victims of dating violence.

WHAT YOU CAN DO TO HELP

Encourage the Development of Healthy Relationships

Experts generally agree that prevention is the best solution to any problem. One prevention effort with regard to dating violence is to encourage teens to develop healthy relationships. The following is a list of tips for talking to teens about this aspect of their lives:

Assess your own relationship values before you talk to kids. How do you expect men and women to act? How should they behave when they disagree? How should decisions be made in a relationship? Make sure that you can explain your reasoning and support it with examples.

Reveal the unspoken "rules of dating." Give kids clear examples of what is appropriate behavior in a dating relationship. Talk to them about the standards of conduct that you expect rather than letting peer talk be their only source of information.

Tell the whole truth, good and bad. Be realistic about the bad things that can happen. Let young people know that violence is never acceptable. Give them a few suggestions or phrases to help them get out of difficult situations: "I'm not ready to go that far," or "I'm not comfortable, can we talk about this?"

Teach assertiveness, not aggressiveness. One of the best skills we can teach teens is to make their feelings known by stating their opinions, desires, and reactions clearly. For example, if they don't want to do something, they need to say so. When there is a conflict, if things cannot be settled, encourage them to always take a break and cool down before feelings get hurt.

Teach anger control. Help kids recognize their personal warning signs for anger. Do they have clenched fists, gritted teeth, tensed shoulders? Teach them to calm down by counting backward, breathing deeply, visualizing a peaceful scene, reassuring themselves that they are in control, or walking away. (Note: Dating violence is not an issue of anger. Anger is a feeling; abuse is a decision to exert power and control over another person.)

Teach problem solving. When a teen is confronted with a tough choice, have him think about several different ways in which it can be resolved and the consequences of each of the alternatives.

Teach negotiation. Help teens understand that compromise and taking turns are positive steps to a healthy relationship and that violence, threats, and insults have no place in respectful negotiation. Teach teens to negotiate and acknowledge the situation. State each person's view honestly and discuss options that allow both people to "win."

Explain the "danger zone." Teach teens to recognize that thoughts of aggression are signs of frustration that need to be acknowledged and dealt with. Help teens understand that any incident of violence in a relationship is an indicator of a serious problem and that such occurrences are likely not only to continue but also to escalate.

Keep no secrets. Secrecy that isolates kids from friends and family is not acceptable and can be the first sign of manipulation and coercion. Teach teens that being strong means relying on the appropriate authorities, from guardians and teachers to the police, if necessary.

Be the ultimate role model. Kids learn from observing those around them. It is critical that you respect yourself, your partner, and other people.[2]

Be Aware of the Warning Signs for Teen Dating Violence

Adolescence often includes changes in a youth's appearance, emotions, and relationships. These changes can make it difficult to differentiate adolescent development from the warning signs of dating violence. If a teen exhibits any of the following warning signs, be mindful that they may not necessarily indicate abuse, but rather normal teen development. Having said this, it is also important not to minimize these warning signs. The warning signs of someone who is in an abusive dating relationship include, but are not limited to, the following:

- Change in behavior when with dating partner—more submissive, withdrawn body language, appearance of dependence on partner

- Makes apologies for partner's behaviors: "He's not possessive, he's just likes to know where I am all the time because he cares."

- Displays worry/fear about making her partner upset

- Doesn't speak freely when his partner is nearby

- Change in appearance, including weight, or wearing clothes with increased body coverage (possibly hiding bruising)

- Provides explanations for injuries or lack of involvement that don't seem truthful

- Starts to use drugs or alcohol

- Decreases involvement in academics

- Excessive thoughts and concerns about the person she dates

- Decrease in time spent with friends and after-school activities[3]

If You Suspect Teen Dating Violence

How you address your concerns about abuse is guided by your agency, professional license, and local laws. Our recommendations are general guidelines for anyone who suspects a teen's partner is abusive.

Choose a private and neutral place to bring up your concerns. Refrain from sharing your concerns about teen dating violence in front of other youth—particularly the partner you believe is abusive. People in abusive relationships often feel ashamed and embarrassed about their experience; removing others from the conversation may lighten the burden of embarrassment. Choose a location that is nonthreatening to the teen.

Be clear and specific about your concerns. As you know, comments like, "He's a jerk" rarely help anyone. Rather than making judgmental statements about someone's partner, share the specific reasons you are concerned.

Release yourself from preconceived notions of how the conversation will go. Don't assume that she will leave the abusive relationship if you show your concern, or, conversely, assume that she will never leave him. Enter into your conversation with empathy and understanding for the victim. Most women and girls who have experienced abuse continue to be with their partners; the time when people leave abusive relationships depends on many things, such as their support systems, resources, and self-worth. Victims stay in abusive relationships for many reasons (review these reasons, provided in the Domestic Violence chapter on page 54). The power of fear, isolation, and loss of self-confidence makes it incredibly difficult to leave abusive partners. Be sensitive to these realities.

Do not force a disclosure. Refrain from bombarding teens with questions about their relationships. Our concern for a teen's safety may lend itself to a desire to know as much as possible so we can best help, but overwhelming her with questions rarely results in a disclosure and can harm your relationship. Learning about the dynamics of an abusive relationship can help us understand why it can be difficult for victims to disclose their experiences and why people stay in the relationship.

Be aware of thoughts and statements that blame the victim. Abusers are responsible for their abusive behaviors. Comments like, "What did you do?" "Did you make him mad?" and "I can't believe you went back to him," imply the victim has responsibility for the abuse. Nothing a victim does justifies abuse. Refrain from making any comments that imply the victim is at fault, because she isn't. The only behaviors we control are our own.

Let the young person know that abuse is the fault of the abuser. It is common that an abuser will blame the victim for his abusive behaviors. Let the victim know she is not to blame, and because she is not responsible for the abusive behaviors she cannot change them. Remind her that simply changing her own behaviors, such as accommodating to the rules of the relationship as defined by the abuser, will not result in the violence going away, because the problem rests *within* the abuser. Let her know you are concerned that the abuse will continue and potentially become more dangerous and damaging.

Refer the youth to a counselor. Providing contact information for an agency, particularly one that specializes in abuse prevention, without forcing the youth to call lets her know how to get in touch with help. If your community is without an abuse resource center, give teens the phone number for the National Teen Dating Abuse Helpline: 866-331-9474; TTY: 866-331-8453.

Refrain from telling a victim what to do. As difficult as it may be, limit your words to letting the teen know you are concerned for her safety and that she deserves a life free from abuse. Send a message of empowerment rather than directives that she must leave the relationship. Telling a youth to end a relationship (i.e., telling her what to do or when to do it) is doing what the abuser is doing: controlling her. Support the teen's ability to make her own decisions while clearly stating your concerns.

Discuss safety. Make a safety plan with the adolescent, even if she states that she will remain in the relationship. A safety plan can open her up to choices she may be unaware of, such as teen dating-abuse counseling, support groups, and legal protection (like a restraining order).

Focus on the person's strengths. Dating abuse often involves denigration of one's self-worth. Constantly being sent messages that you are a "lesser" person can result in believing that your needs and desires are less important than other people's. Remind the teen of her gifts and strengths and find opportunities to put these gifts to use.

RESOURCES

Break the Cycle (breakthecycle.org). Offers curriculum and videos on teens speaking out against dating violence, downloadable handouts on dating violence, and online quiz for teens to see if their relationship is healthy.

Choose Respect (chooserespect.org). Includes materials and downloads for use by parents and teachers.

Love Is Not Abuse (loveisnotabuse.com).

National Coalition Against Domestic Violence/Teen Dating Violence Project (ncadv.org). Phone: 303-839-1852.

National Teen Dating Abuse Helpline.
Phone: 866-331-9474, TTY: 866-331-8453.

Preventing Teen Dating Violence: A Three-Session Curriculum for Teaching Adolescents by Carole Sousa. New York: Dating Violence Prevention Project, 1989.

Date Violence by Elaine Landau. New York: Franklin Watts, 2004.

Dating Violence: Young Women in Danger by Barrie Levy. Seattle, WA: Seal Press, 1991.

The Verbally Abusive Relationship: How to Recognize It and How to Respond by Patricia Evans. Holbrook, MA: Adams Media Corporation, 1996.

NOTES

1. Teenage Research Unlimited commissioned by Liz Claiborne Inc. (conducted March 2006), *Liz Claiborne Inc. Topline Findings: Teen Relationship Abuse Survey* (Northbrook: IL), loveisnotabuse.com/surveyresults_2007mstr .htm (accessed September 24, 2007).

2. Liz Claiborne Women's Work, *A Parent's Handbook: How to Talk to Your Children about Developing Healthy Relationships.* Booklet. N.p.

3. Rape and Abuse Crisis Center of Fargo/Moorhead, *Danger Ahead: Early Warning Signs of Teen Dating Violence.* (2005). Booklet. N.p.

DANGER AHEAD!

EARLY WARNING SIGNS OF TEEN DATING VIOLENCE

Does Your Partner:

- Isolate you from people you care about most or from friends you had before you began dating?

- Call you names and put you down? OR Put you on a pedestal and say things like "I don't deserve you"?

- Frequently embarrass or make fun of you in front of other people? OR Ignore you or your feelings?

- Use intimidation to make you do what he wants?

- Make you feel you cannot disagree with her and there is no way out the relationship?

- Make you perform sexual acts that you don't enjoy?

- Threaten you with force, words, or weapons?

- Use alcohol or drugs as an excuse for saying hurtful things or abusing you?

- Not believe he has hurt you or blames you for what he has done?

- Get extremely angry and you don't know why?

- Physically force you to do what you do not want to do?

- Get jealous of your other relationships and accuse you of being with others when you do not call?

DEPRESSION

Depression can be described as a persistent state of sadness, loss of interest in pleasurable things, and a general feeling of hopelessness. Clinical or major depression is very different from everyday ups and downs or feeling occasionally sad. Depression interferes with our ability to work, go to school, and participate in activities. Depression can also affect our relationships with others. Major depression is a mental illness that can and should be treated.

Signs and Symptoms of Depression

When a person is diagnosed with depression, typically some of the predominant symptoms are sadness, emptiness, and feelings of hopelessness. Someone with depression may experience weight loss or weight gain without intentionally dieting or overeating. People who are depressed may also suffer from insomnia or hypersomnia (sleeping too much). Someone who is depressed may feel exhausted and drained of energy and sluggish almost every day. People who are depressed may experience focus and concentration problems; one sign of this in children and adolescents is falling grades. Other symptoms include irritability and grouchiness, and strong feelings of guilt and self-hatred. People experiencing depression may also have headaches or stomach problems.

Sometimes depression in teens looks like what some may consider "normal adolescent behavior," but be careful not to assume this is the case. Depression can look different in children and adolescents than it does in adults. While the predominant symptom in adults is often sadness, the predominant symptom or mood in an adolescent with depression may be irritability and grouchiness. A teen who is depressed may be quick to anger and easily irritated. She may seem oversensitive and be disagreeable with others. It is important not to credit this mood to a teen's acting out because she is not getting her way.[1] Teens with depression may withdraw from friends and family and appear to have changes in their personalities. While the teen years are often times of emotional ups and downs, it is a persistent pattern of negative moods, coupled with the signs below, that signals depression.

People who are depressed cannot just "snap out of it." Depression often distorts a person's thinking and makes him feel more pessimistic and hopeless than seems normal or appropriate for the situation. This unclear thinking can be one factor that leads a person to consider suicide (see page 111 for a more complete discussion on suicide).

Why Do People Become Depressed?

There is no known specific cause of depression, but several factors can put people at risk for this disease. These risk factors include a family history of depression, ongoing medical issues, and underlying personality and emotional factors. Other risk factors include lower socioeconomic status, lack of social support, and recent or severe life stressors. People who are depressed earlier in life are at a higher risk of more frequent and more severe episodes of depression later in life. While there are people who have more risk factors than others, depression can strike anyone.

Girls are at a much higher risk for depression than boys. During childhood, girls and boys experience fairly equal rates of depression, but this ratio increases to two girls with depression for every boy with depression during adolescence.[2] Female teens with depression are twice as likely as their male counterparts to attempt suicide.[3] Social factors and changes in peer relationships for girls during adolescence are thought to contribute to this increase in depression.

Low self-esteem is often both a cause and consequence of depression. People with a poor self-image are more susceptible to depression, and poor self-image often is exacerbated by depression. Teens are under a great deal of pressure to be "the best." There is pressure from friends, family, and society to be the prettiest, the strongest, the smartest, the thinnest, and the most popular. These enormous pressures can lead to low self-esteem, and the distorted thinking that is linked to depression can make these pressures seem insurmountable.

Problems Associated with Untreated Depression

Teens who are depressed are at risk for problems at school, at home, and in their social circles. Depression can lead to lower grades and poor school attendance. Teens with depression may also run away from home and engage in high-risk behaviors like unsafe sex. Teens who are depressed are at a higher risk for becoming unwed parents. People with depression are at a higher risk for drug and alcohol abuse, usually due to "self-medicating" in an attempt to alleviate the suffering caused by the symptoms of depression.[4]

Teens who are depressed may also engage in self-injurious behavior and violence toward others. Participating in self-injurious behaviors to alleviate the pain of depression is an increasingly common coping skill used by adolescents. For a more complete discussion about self-injury, see the chapter on page 101. Violence at schools and campuses is also on the rise; teens who have lashed out at class-mates and peers at school have all shown evidence of depression.

The most severe consequence of untreated depression is suicide. People with depression are at a high risk for suicidal thoughts and behaviors. These thoughts and attempts at suicide must be taken very seriously.

It's important to remember that depression is treatable and in some cases even preventable. The next sections of this chapter discuss how you can help a teen who may be depressed and what teens can do if they think they are depressed.

> "I think teens are good at hiding depression. Adults need to be more aware of the signs. If someone at my school would have been more aware, maybe it wouldn't have been so hard. I don't know that we can entirely rely on parents to see the signs—they're blinded by being the parent. It could have been as simple as someone asking if I was feeling down. Just that could have helped get the ball rolling to me getting help." —Drew

WHAT YOU CAN DO TO HELP

If you suspect you or someone you know is depressed, it is critical to talk about it and get help. Because many physical illnesses can have symptoms similar to those of depression, it is important to seek medical attention. Medical professionals can run tests to determine if there is a physical cause to the symptoms of depression. If other physical aliments are ruled out and a diagnosis of depression is given, medication may be prescribed. Many people with depression also receive help from counseling and therapy. Once appropriate medical help and counseling have been sought, there are many things you can do to support teens with depression.

Communicate

Opening the lines of communication is essential. Let the teen know you care and offer your support and your time. Ask how he is doing and listen without asking too many questions. Be persistent in offering a listening ear. Teens in general may be hesitant to engage with an adult, and hesitancy is even more likely when a teen is depressed. Continually offering your support will let him know you are interested in hearing about what is going on in his life. When a teen opens up to you, listen more than talk, and validate his feelings.

When talking to a teen about depression, remembering where she is developmentally and culturally is vital to understanding her experience. Watch teen shows, read teen magazines, and look at favorite teen Internet sites to get an idea of how different the teen world is from the adult world.

Offer Your Time

Even if a teen is receiving professional help, stay involved with him and his treatment progress. Don't insist on details or ask him to talk about his depression until he is ready; simply be available to spend time with him. You can start short conversations or engage with him in an activity of his choosing, such as taking a walk or grabbing a bite to eat. The activity is not as important as the offering of your time.

Encourage Peer Support and Engagement

Don't let teens isolate themselves. Encourage peer activities and social pursuits. Look for opportunities that might interest the teen, including concerts, sporting events, community education classes, or other activities. Offer transportation to events when possible, or if you are a parent or guardian offer to have friends to your house.

Encourage Physical Activity

Exercise is a great way to alleviate the symptoms of depression. Exercise does not have to be intense and can involve you or other family members. Going on a walk or riding a bike are simple ways of getting exercise. If you join the teen on a walk, this is also a great time to talk in a nuetral environment.

RESOURCES

American Counseling Association (counseling.org). The official Web site of the American Counseling Association. Resources and information on where to find a counselor are provided.

Covenant House Nineline. Phone: 800-999-9999. A 24-hour hotline to talk about concerns such as abuse, suicide, and running away.

Mental Health America (www1.nmha.org). Basic information about the symptoms and treatment of depression.

National Alliance on Mental Illness (nami.org). A grassroots organization that aims to improve the lives of people with mental illness.

Understanding Teenage Depression: A Guide to Diagnosis, Treatment, and Management by Maureen Empfield and Nicholas Bakalar. New York: Henry Holt, 2001.

When Nothing Matters Anymore: A Survival Guide for Depressed Teens by Bev Cobain, Peter Jensen, and Elizabeth Verdick. Minneapolis: Free Spirit Publishing, 2007.

NOTES

1. American Psychiatric Association Staff, *Diagnostic and Statistical Manual of Mental Disorders*, 4th ed., text revision (Washington, DC: American Psychiatric Association, 2000).

2. R. J. Hazler and E. A. Mellin, "The Developmental Origins and Treatment Needs of Female Adolescents with Depression," *Journal of Counseling and Development* 82 (2004): 18–24.

3. R. P. Stanard, "Assessment and Treatment of Adolescent Depression and Suicidality," *Journal of Mental Health Counseling* 22 (2000): 204–217.

4. Ibid.

Signs and Symptoms of Depression*

- Sad, depressed, or irritable

- Loss of pleasure or interest in most activities

- Significant weight loss or weight gain

- Sleeping too much or not being able to sleep

- Feeling restless or feelings of being slowed down

- Loss of energy and fatigue almost every day

- Feeling worthless or excessively guilty

- Inability to think, concentrate, or make decisions (this may result in falling grades)

- Recurrent thoughts of death or dying, thinking about killing oneself

- Aches and pains like headaches, stomachaches, and diarrhea

* Symptoms not attributable to drug or alcohol use, a medical condition, or better accounted for by grief after the loss of a loved one.

What Can Teens Do If They Are Depressed?

There are a number of things you can do to help yourself or your friends if you are depressed.

Learn about depression. It is perfectly normal to feel sad, angry, and depressed. Everyone has ups and downs, good days and bad days. It is when the sad feelings or irritation stay with you for weeks that depression might be the cause.

Talk to someone you trust. If you think you or someone you know is depressed, talk to someone about it. It is good to share your feelings with friends, but if you are depressed you should also talk to an adult about it, because they may be able to get you the kind of professional help you need. Remember that parents and adults often don't know enough about depression to know what the symptoms are, especially in kids and teens. Just because an adult you know and care about hasn't asked about your feelings, that doesn't mean he or she doesn't care. Telling an adult you trust about these feelings is an important step toward getting better.

Seek help from a professional. An adult can help you make an appointment with a doctor or counselor.

Don't isolate yourself. People who are depressed often feel like they want to be alone, and no longer enjoy some of the social things they used to. If you are depressed, retreating to your bedroom may seem like the best option, but ultimately it may make you feel worse. Spend time with friends, especially people who are positive and supportive. It is especially important not to be alone when you are thinking about hurting or killing yourself.

Avoid the temptation of excessively playing video games, watching TV or movies, and surfing the Internet, especially by yourself. These are all activities that can increase the time you spend alone and lead to more negative thoughts. If these are your favorite activities, invite a friend to do them with you.

Make healthy choices. People who are depressed may not feel like eating, or may feel like overeating. Making healthy choices with food is important for everybody's health, but needs more attention when someone is depressed. It may be tempting to seek escape through alcohol or drugs, but that may make the depression worse. Staying away from these substances is important all the time, but especially when depression is involved.

Stay physically active. Doing active things can help alleviate the symptoms of depression. If you are feeling depressed, go for a walk or participate in some other physical activity. If you have a friend who is depressed, ask her or him to go for a walk with you.

Remember, you are not alone. Depression does not have to be permanent. You *can* feel better if you reach out to others and seek help.

DIVORCE

It is widely acknowledged that approximately half of all marriages end in divorce, and many of those marriages involve children. Single-parent families and blended families are increasingly commonplace. Despite its prevalence, divorce can have a negative effect on children and teens. This chapter discusses some of the ways divorce affects kids and how you can help ease the pain for children and teens whose families are going through this transition.

Effects of Divorce

Divorce carries with it very real financial consequences. Parents must now finance two homes, which can lead to a drastic reduction in the amount of money available. Teens may have to move into smaller homes, change schools, begin sharing a room when they had not done so previously, and have to reduce the number of or eliminate after-school activities in which they were enrolled. Sometimes the financial consequences of divorce leave children in poverty. Parents may have to return to work after a period spent at home or work longer hours, leaving children in day care or on their own for longer periods of time than before the divorce. Teens may have to adjust to rarely seeing one of the parents because he or she no longer has custody, and may have to adjust to having different relationships with their extended families.

There are also less tangible, but often just as damaging, emotional consequences that follow a divorce. Children can experience a multitude of negative emotions about their parents' divorce: guilt, shame, sadness, worry, and shock.

The breakup of their parents' marriage may come as a surprise to some teens, leaving them with a sense of disbelief. Teens may feel a great deal of anger and loss about the divorce, and may even question whether they are to blame for the situation. Teenagers' brains are still developing, and they sometimes think very differently than adults do; one of these cognitive differences is a tendency to hold themselves responsible somehow for their parents' separation. Teens may have additional worries about divorce, including where they will live and how they will maintain relationships with both parents. The emotional consequences of divorce can continue long after childhood is over. People whose parents are divorced are at an increased risk for psychological problems as adults.[1]

> "My parents got in a big argument when my mom brought me to my dad's and now I feel like I am being forced to choose between them. They want me to decide things they should be deciding together. I hate it when they fight. I don't think they know how stressed out it makes me." —Abby

It is important to note that for many teens, not all feelings regarding their parents' divorce are negative. They may also feel relief or a sense of greater safety, and they may look forward to having a new kind of relationship with each parent. There are times when being away from parents' discord and arguing can improve the mental health of a youth. Sometimes a teen may feel guilty about the sense of relief he feels when his parents divorce.

Even when the divorce makes life easier, teens will likely have mixed feelings about the situation. Each family's transition is unique, but there are some general things that one can do to ease the pain and problems of divorce for teens.

While the focus of this chapter is teens' experiences with divorce, it is important to recognize that there are also emotional consequences for the parents. Parents who are going through the breakup of their relationship are under strain too, sometimes making parenting more difficult as they work through their own transitions.

WHAT YOU CAN DO TO HELP

Every member of a family going through a divorce will need support from caring people. You can play a role in a teen's healthy coping by being supportive and available as a sounding board.

Use Inclusive Language

One thing we can all do to reduce the stigma and shame of divorce is to use inclusive language when speaking about families. A teen may be embarrassed that her parents are divorcing, or feel as if she is the only person going through this. Assuring her that there are all kinds of families can help ease some of this shame. When speaking about parents and families, don't always speak about family as a two-parent, married-parent family. Normalizing the diversity of families can reduce the amount of shame a teen feels about being from a family whose parents are divorced.

Support the Parents

If you are an adult whose friend is going though a divorce, support your friend through the transitions.

Being a sounding board, volunteering to babysit, and offering to find professional help are all ways you can support an adult going through a divorce.

Listen

Talking and listening to teens whose parents are divorcing is a good way to support them in this tough time. Teens may not feel as if they can talk to their parents about the divorce, because the parents are at the center of the issue. Offering an objective, nonjudgmental ear to a teen can help him process what is going on with his family and hopefully normalize some of the feelings he is having.

Teens whose parents are divorcing are at a slightly higher risk for psychological, behavioral, social, and academic problems.[2] If a teen you are working with seems to be having problems adjusting to her parents' divorce, and you are concerned for her mental health, offer to help her connect with a counselor or program, which could help her be more successful as an adult.

RESOURCES

Kidshealth.org (kidshealth.org). Includes tips for teens dealing with divorce.

Young Women's Health (youngwomenshealth.org). Includes suggestions for young women dealing with divorced parents.

The Divorce Helpbook for Teens by Cynthia MacGregor. Atascadero, CA: Impact Publishers, 2004.

Help! A Girl's Guide to Divorce and Stepfamilies by Nancy Holyoke. Middleton, WI: Pleasant Company Publications, 1999.

Now What Do I Do? A Guide to Help Teenagers with Their Parents' Separation or Divorce by Lynn Cassella-Kapusinski. Skokie, IL: ACTA Publications, 2006.

NOTES

1. P. R. Amato and J. M. Sobolewski, "The Effects of Divorce and Marital Discord on Adult Children's Psychological Well-Being," *American Sociological Review* 66 (2001): 900–921.

2. P. R. Amato, "Children of Divorce in the 1990s: An Update of the Amato and Keith (1991) Meta-Analysis," *Journal of Family Psychology* 15 (2001): 355–370.

Things Parents Can Do to
Help a Teen Dealing with Divorce

- Join with your spouse to tell your kids about the divorce together.

- Share with your teens brief, honest, and developmentally appropriate information about the situation. This is not a time for blaming.

- Maintain consistent parenting roles and expectations—don't let guilt make you do things you normally wouldn't.

- Continue to co-parent and communicate with your ex-spouse about parenting issues.

- Be there to talk and listen—be proactive about talking to teens about what has happened. Your teen is probably dealing with conflicting emotions such as sadness, guilt, anger, worry, and relief—sometimes all at once. Be willing to talk about these feelings together.

- Dealing with a new school, a new home, or a new economic situation is difficult for both teens and parents. Do what you can to make the transition as easy as possible for all of you.

- *Don't* put your teen in the middle of arguments with your ex-spouse.

- *Don't* say bad things about each other or argue in front of your teen.

- *Don't* ask your teen to spy on the other parent, or ask your teen questions about your ex's personal life.

- *Don't* use your teen as a go-between. Communicate maturely and directly with your spouse.

Reprinted with permission from *Helping Teens Handle Tough Experiences: Strategies to Foster Resilience,* by Jill Nelson and Sarah Kjos. Copyright © 2008 by Search Institute®, Minneapolis, Minnesota, 800-888-7828, www.search-institute.org. All rights reserved.

DOMESTIC VIOLENCE

Domestic violence is one of the best-kept secrets in America. One in four American women report they have been physically abused by a husband or boyfriend at some point in their lives; nearly one third of all Americans say they know a woman who has been physically abused by her husband or boyfriend in the past year.[1] While these statistics speak to the staggering prevalence of domestic violence, our media and education systems often fail to highlight the significance of this issue.

"I remember constantly being complimented on what a perfect family we had. People would say my parents could write books on parenting, but people didn't know what went on behind closed doors. People didn't know my real family. When people said these things, it made the domestic violence an even bigger secret." —JoAnne

According to the U.S. Department of Justice, between 1998 and 2002, 84 percent of spouse-abuse victims were female, and 86 percent of victims of dating-partner abuse were female.[2] To reflect this reality, we have chosen to refer to adult victims of domestic violence as "she" and perpetrators as "he," but it is important to recognize that women can also be perpetrators of domestic violence, and that domestic violence happens in all types of relationships, including married, dating, heterosexual, and homosexual partnerships.

Domestic violence is not about disagreement, and it's not simply an issue of anger. Domestic violence is one partner exerting power and control over the other, in ways that range from economic control to physical abuse. In homes where there is domestic violence, children are frequently victims of abuse as well. Even if a teen is not physically abused by the perpetrator of domestic violence, the emotional effects of witnessing domestic violence are often comparable to experiencing personal abuse.

Use the handout on page 58 to understand what domestic violence is and the many ways perpetrators of domestic violence take power and control over their partners. Share this handout with peers, co-workers, and people whose welfare you are concerned about.

WHAT YOU CAN DO TO HELP

If You Feel Discomfort Talking about Domestic Violence

If you are uncomfortable talking about domestic violence, explore these questions: Is it because you need more information on the dynamics of domestic violence? Does it feel too close to home because you or someone you care for has experienced domestic violence? Do you think women who stay in abusive relationships are just as much to blame as the abuser for exposing their children to abuse? Take the risk of being completely honest with your biases and discomforts and seek evidence-based information on domestic violence to address your concerns.

Believe the Teen

Youth almost never lie about abuse. If a teen discloses abuse in the home, let him know you believe him. Never underestimate the power of your support. Recognize the courage that led to his disclosure and commend him for it. Encourage the teen to say as much as he wants to about what has happened. Listen without judgment.

Discuss Safety

Ask the teen if she feels safe and if it is safe for her to return home. Be aware that youth may minimize the abuse or feel the need to protect their families. Minimizing the abuse may be due to fear of social service involvement, feeling responsible for the abuse in the home, or not wanting to break the family apart. Determine whether you need to contact your local social service agency, and if so, make a report immediately. Different states and municipalities have different definitions of what constitutes abuse and neglect; find out if you have to report domestic violence to a child protective services agency. Document what the teen shared with you, regardless of whether or not you have a responsibility to report to authorities.

Make a basic safety plan with the youth if he plans to return home. Assist him in identifying what he can do if domestic violence occurs. A basic plan might include something like this:

- Call 911.
- If a fight begins, move to the safest place in your home (try to move to a room with an exit, and avoid rooms with weapons, such as the kitchen).

- If you can leave, go to a neighbor's home, and call 911 from there.
- Practice getting out of your home safely; identify which windows/doors provide the safest exit.

Validate the Teen's Feelings

Providing youth with a nonjudgmental and safe space to express their feelings is critical. Simply ask, "How do you feel about what is going on in your home?" Be aware of common emotions of teens living in homes with domestic violence, such as fear, shame, guilt, isolation, helplessness, embarrassment, anxiety, and anger. Accept the youth's feelings, even if they make you uncomfortable. If a teen shares that she loves the person who is abusive, validate this feeling; don't try to challenge the feelings she holds.

Be Aware That Any Youth Could Be Exposed to Domestic Violence

Domestic violence occurs in all types of communities and homes. Domestic violence occurs in families from all backgrounds, religions, and socioeconomic status, and in both heterosexual and homosexual relationships. People in abusive relationships often say the abuser "behaves like a different person when other people are around" and can seem very likable to others. Just because a family is actively involved with their children's school or activities does not necessarily mean there could not be domestic violence in the home. A compliant and enjoyable parent or guardian may behave in other ways in the home.

Respect the Teen's Difficulty in Learning to Trust

While not all young people who live in homes where domestic violence is present develop an inability to trust, many do. Let the youth take the lead in defining your relationship with each other. Practicing patience when you are concerned for a youth's safety is challenging: we often just want the youth to disclose enough information so we can report to the authorities, who can make change happen. Respect the teen's protection of what happens in his home and don't give up on your relationship, even when you feel you're being pushed away.

Be Aware of the Emotional Impact of Living with Domestic Violence

The more aware you are of the common thoughts and emotions of teens living with domestic violence, the better able you are to understand where these emotions stem from and how you can help normalize these feelings for teens. As with all issues, being a primary and/or secondary victim of abuse impacts teens differently. In general, youth who witness domestic violence may feel:

Powerless for being unable to stop the abuse and violence from happening to their parent or themselves

Guilty for loving the abuser; blaming themselves for causing the abuse

Angry with the abuser for hurting them and their family; for having to move to a shelter

Confused by having mixed feelings of love/hate toward the abuser; by not understanding why the abuser does this when he claims to love Mom and the family; by not understanding why Mom stays; by parents trying to get children to choose sides

Afraid for their safety and that of their parents; of being hurt; of losing someone they love; of abandonment

Isolated by feeling alone; by feeling that this is only happening to their family

Anxious because of constant worry due to the uncertainty of when abuse will occur; when the abuser is angry

Sad that this is happening; that their parents are repeatedly hurt

Ashamed of the secrets in their homes[3]

Become Aware of the Many Signs and Effects of Domestic Violence

Children and teens can be affected in many ways by domestic violence. This is a general list of signs and effects that teens may exhibit or keep to themselves:

- Stress-related physical ailments such as headaches or stomachaches
- Difficulty concentrating in school and/or preoccupation with concerns at home
- Low self-esteem, fear of doing wrong, fear of expressing emotions
- Overachievement, feeling the need to be perfect
- Isolation, feeling different from others, feeling pressure to keep family "secrets," feeling unable to have friends over
- Believing in and/or employing violence as an acceptable means to resolve problems and express anger (e.g., physical fights, destroying property, harm to animals)
- Identification with the abuser, as a youth believes it is safer to be the abuser than the victim; copying abuser's behavior
- Identification with the victim, being passive and submissive, not expressing who they are
- Aggressive language or behavior, preoccupation with violence, associating love with violence
- Post-traumatic stress disorder (PTSD)
- Running away repeatedly
- Fear of abandonment
- Withdrawing from peer relationships
- Elevated fear, anxiety, depression, or loneliness, even when in a safe environment
- Thoughts of suicide[4]

Emphasize the Responsibility of the Abuser

Domestic violence is a choice made by the abuser. Be aware of thoughts you may be having toward the primary victim—most often the adult female—and refrain from making any victim-blaming statements. For example, "It's awful that your mom has you in that situation" implies that this is a situation the mom can easily escape and is responsible for. Again, with any form of abuse, the sole responsibility lies with the abuser. Be careful to avoid asking a youth to modify his behaviors to meet the demands of the abuser; it implies that the youth "just needs to listen." Seek continued education on domestic violence to better understand the dynamics of intimate-partner violence.

Use Curriculum That Teaches Kids about Domestic Violence

The environment we grow up in can naturally become our view of what is acceptable. Domestic violence is never "normal," okay, or acceptable. Use language and curriculum with teens that address domestic violence. Let youth know that no one, no matter what has happened, has the right to mistreat them. Ideas for programming include bringing in speakers from local agencies that work with domestic violence issues; including programming or activities specific to Domestic Violence Awareness Month every October; and using the "I Wish the Hitting Would Stop" education program, available at redflaggreenflag.com.

Set Clear Expectations for Nonviolent Behavior and Language in Your Program

Modeling nonviolent behavior can help teens define appropriate norms. Provide clear information, both written and verbal, to all youth and adults regarding the expectations for behavior in your program or setting. Explain prior to participation what is deemed acceptable and unacceptable behavior and language, and the consequences for harmful behavior and language. If a teen violates the expectations, explain why it is unacceptable.

RESOURCES

Family Violence Prevention Fund's Action Line. Phone: 800-END-ABUSE.

National Domestic Violence Hotline. Phone: 800-799- SAFE.

National Coalition Against Domestic Violence (nrcdv.org). Phone: 303-839-1852.

A Child's Guide to Surviving in a Troubled Family: Breakthrough Strategies to Teach and Counsel Troubled Youth by Ruth Herman Wells. Woodburn, OR: Youth Change, 1993.

Family Violence in the United States: Defining, Understanding, and Combating Abuse by Denise A. Hines and Kathleen Malley-Morrison. Thousand Oaks, CA: Sage Publications, 2005.

When Something Feels Wrong: A Survival Guide about Abuse for Young People by Deanna S. Pledge. Minneapolis, MN: Free Spirit Publishing, 2003.

When Violence Begins at Home: A Comprehensive Guide to Understanding and Ending Domestic Abuse by K. J. Wilson. Alameda, CA: Hunter House, 2006.

NOTES

1. Lieberman Research Inc., *Domestic Violence Advertising Campaign Tracking Survey* (Wave IV), conducted for the Advertising Council and the Family Violence Prevention Fund, 1994.

2. M. R. Durose, C. Wolf Harlow, P. A. Langan, M. Motivans, R. R. Rantala, and E. L. Smith, *Bureau of Justice Statistics, Family Violence Statistics: Including Statistics on Strangers and Acquaintances* (Washington, DC: U.S. Department of Justice, 2005), www.ojp.usdoj-gov/bjs/pub/pdf/fvs.pdf (accessed September 6, 2007).

3. Houston County Women's Resources, *Caught in the Middle: The Effects of Domestic Violence on Children*. (1995). Booklet. N.p.

4. Rape & Abuse Crisis Center, Fargo-Moorhead, *Children Living in Homes with Domestic Violence*. (2007). Booklet. N.p.

The Power and Control Wheel

The Power and Control Wheel was developed by battered women in Duluth, Minnesota, who had been abused by their male partners and were attending women's education groups sponsored by the women's shelter. The wheel used in this curriculum is for men who have used violence against their female partners. Each segment of the wheel describes a way in which an abuser can exert power over his victim. The wheel is designed to serve as a visual reference and reminder of the ways abuse can manifest and the reasons why it persists. While we recognize that there are women who use violence against men, and that there are men and women in same-sex relationships who use violence, this wheel is meant specifically to illustrate men's abusive behaviors toward women.

Domestic Abuse Intervention Project • 202 East Superior Street • Duluth, Minnesota 55802 • 218-722-2781 • www.duluth-model.org

EATING DISORDERS

Eating disorders are among the most prevalent mental illnesses in the United States today. Estimates of the number of people suffering from eating disorders range from two million[1] to ten million.[2] Eating disorders are much more common in females, but they can occur in males as well. The common symptoms of all eating disorders are severely disturbed eating behaviors and patterns. Anyone whose thoughts about eating, weight, or body image control a significant portion of her or his life may have an eating disorder.

TYPES OF EATING DISORDERS

Anorexia Nervosa

Anorexia is an eating disorder in which a person has an intense fear of gaining weight. People with anorexia are unable to maintain a healthy or normal body weight: their body weight drops below the minimum required for their height and age. People with anorexia deny that their low weight is a problem and develop distorted views of how their bodies look. They will often see bulges, curves, or fat where there are none.[3] For a female to be diagnosed with anorexia, she will have stopped having menstrual periods for at least three months.

There are two types of anorexia: restricting and binge eating/purging. People with the restricting type of anorexia eat extremely limited amounts of calories, fast, and/or exercise excessively. People with the binge eating/purging type of anorexia may eat large quantities of food, but then purge it from their bodies by vomiting and/or using laxatives, diuretics, or enemas. Some people with this type of anorexia will not eat large quantities of food, but will participate in purging behaviors after ingesting a very small amount of calories.

> "I just wish things were different. I know I should eat, but I can't. I felt like no one understood that my life would just be perfect if I weighed 72 lbs. Everyone argued about that with me and I knew in my head that it probably wasn't true, but I felt in my heart it was true. I wished people would just leave me and my weight alone. It's not their business! I really thought if I could just be 72 lbs, I would be fine." —Lori

Bulimia Nervosa

Bulimia is the most common eating disorder.[4] People with bulimia will have several recurring episodes of eating extremely large amounts of food in a short time. This quantity is significantly more than most people would eat in the same circumstances, and not something like overeating at a holiday meal. As a person with bulimia consumes these large quantities of food, she feels out of control and unable to stop what she is doing.[5] After bingeing, the person will take extreme measures to prevent weight gain by purging the food from her body. These measures might include vomiting, taking laxatives, using enemas, exercising excessively, or fasting. For a person to be diagnosed with bulimia, these bingeing and purging cycles must happen, on average, at least twice a week for at least three months. Bulimia is different from the binge eating/purging type of anorexia because people with bulimia often maintain a healthy weight.

Eating Disorder Not Otherwise Specified

People may have many of the symptoms of anorexia and bulimia, but they may not have all of them. When this is the case, a person may be diagnosed with "eating disorder—not otherwise specified" (eating disorder NOS).[6] For example, a girl may have all the symptoms of anorexia but still have her menstrual periods, or a young man may have lost an extreme amount of weight due to anorexia, but is still in the normal body-weight range; both of these situations are examples of when a person would be diagnosed with eating disorder NOS. Other types of eating disorder NOS include binge eating disorder, wherein a person participates in binge eating but does not purge, and compulsive overeating.

ABOUT EATING DISORDERS

Warning Signs and Symptoms of Eating Disorders

Some of the more obvious signs and symptoms of an eating disorder are extreme weight loss, and dieting or not eating. People with eating disorders will go to great lengths to hide their illness, so it is important to be aware of some of the other symptoms and behaviors that people with eating disorders have.

Physical symptoms beyond weight loss may be present in someone with an eating disorder. These symptoms include thinning of hair and drying of skin, easy bruising, and lanugo (fine downy hair that appears on the face, arms, and torso). People with eating disorders may also have a sore throat, tooth decay, and intestinal problems such as constipation or diarrhea. There may be cuts, scratches, or calluses on the back of the hand—these are caused by a person's teeth when manually inducing vomiting. Because of a lowered body temperature, fingers and toes may have a blue tint. People with eating disorders have difficulty concentrating, may exhibit confusion, and have trouble making decisions. There are also several physical symptoms that can only be detected with medical tests: slowed heart rate, low blood sugar, and low blood pressure.

People with eating disorders also exhibit common behavioral patterns. Behaviors to be aware of include not eating (or making excuses not to eat or be present at mealtimes) and overeating. You may also notice rituals about food, or cutting up food and never actually eating it, or just moving food around on the plate. Other behaviors to look for are trips to the bathroom immediately after meals or snacks, hoarding or hiding food, and wearing baggy or bulky clothing.

Teens who were once vibrant may seem detached, aloof, and depressed. They may obsess about their weight and bodies. They may become suicidal and display self-hatred. They may be more isolated from friends and no longer want to participate in events—especially events involving eating or food.

Not all people with eating disorders are extremely thin. As noted earlier, people who have bulimia can maintain a healthy weight, while people with binge eating disorder or compulsive overeating disorder may be overweight to morbidly obese.

It is important not to wait to intervene until someone meets all of the diagnostic criteria for an eating disorder. If you even suspect a young person has any of the symptoms of these eating disorders, arrange for help!

Causes of Eating Disorders

Eating disorders are about much more than weight or food: they are complex mental health issues. There is no one clear-cut cause of an eating disorder, but there are factors that contribute to the likelihood of developing one. Peer culture has a great deal of influence over adolescents, especially when it comes to body image. This outside influence can be one of the greatest risk factors for developing an eating disorder. Persons who are teased by others about their bodies and their weight have a higher risk of developing an eating disorder.[7]

Social pressures and the popular culture contribute to engaging in disordered eating behaviors. Magazines, TV, movies, and all sorts of media stress the importance of being thin and pretty. Models and actresses are often extremely thin and set a standard that is unattainable for most women—especially those who want to be healthy. Adolescents tend to be quite impressionable, and fitting in is very important to them. Wanting to be as thin as these role models can cause adolescents to develop image problems and eventually an eating disorder.

There are also emotional and psychological factors associated with the development of an eating disorder. These include low self-esteem and poor coping skills. Adolescents and others with eating disorders may have a poor self-concept and feel bad about themselves. They may have a pessimistic view not only of their bodies, but also of who they are as people. People with eating disorders may have never learned proper coping skills for dealing with feelings. They may have difficulties expressing their feelings, especially those feelings that are viewed as negative. People who are at risk for developing an eating disorder may have been physically or sexually abused.

There is evidence that eating disorders run in families, and there is an increased risk for developing anorexia if someone in your immediate biological family has had or currently has an eating disorder. There is also evidence that links family members with eating disorders to the development of other mood disorders, such as depression.[8]

Beyond biology, there are other family factors that increase the risk of developing an eating disorder. Families that have poor communication skills and poor support within the family create an environment that may lead to the development of an eating disorder in a family member. Adolescents whose parents have extreme eating habits and a preoccupation with food and dieting may be more at risk of developing an eating disorder.[9]

Sometimes a stressful or traumatic event can trigger an eating disorder.[10] Eating disorders can start when someone diets and loses a lot of weight; the habits can be hard to break and eventually become increasingly important, developing into an eating disorder. Some athletes are at an increased risk for developing an eating disorder. Sports like ballet, wrestling, and gymnastics place a large amount of focus on weight and size. Adolescents participating in these or other sports may feel extra pressure to be thin.

WHAT YOU CAN DO TO HELP

Medical Help

The most important thing to do if you suspect someone has an eating disorder is to help him seek medical treatment, involving the parents or guardians when required. Eating disorders (especially anorexia) can be fatal. People with advanced eating disorders may develop permanent heart problems and dangerously imbalanced blood electrolyte levels. They may be dehydrated and severely malnourished. Eating disorders can also lead to kidney problems, dental problems, and osteoporosis. If an eating disorder develops in adolescence, growth may be stunted. Girls with anorexia may develop fertility problems. Menstruation may stop and puberty may be delayed.

Counseling and Therapy

For a person with an eating disorder, counseling, along with medical treatment, is essential to overcoming the disease: weight and attitudes toward food are merely symptoms of a mental illness with deep-rooted emotional causes. A teen with an eating disorder may require individual, group, and family counseling. Each type of counseling is important and serves to confront different problems associated with eating disorders. Individual counseling can help with underlying self-esteem and mood issues. Group therapy is completed with other people with eating disorders. People can learn a great deal about their illness and recovery from those who have eating disorders as well. Family therapy is important to address some of the issues in the family that may have led to or allowed the eating disorder. It can also be a source of support for parents who are at a loss about how to help their child.

Open Communication and Support

Talking to a teen about his eating disorder may be difficult. Eating disorders thrive on secrecy, and most likely the person with the eating disorder will go to great lengths to deny that there is a problem. Approach him in a nonthreatening and nonblaming way. Emphasize your concern rather than his "bad behavior," but don't be afraid to talk plainly about vomiting, bingeing, or other behaviors that need to be demystified. These possible communication difficulties should not stop you from trying to get help for the young person. Expect denial and insist on medical and other professional help anyway.

It is important to build a support system around the person with an eating disorder. This should include professional helpers (medical practitioners and mental health practitioners), as well as family members, trusted adults, and friends. This support should include focusing on internal beauty rather than outside appearance. Praise the young person for her intrinsic value, not weight gains or losses or looking pretty. It is important for the teen to participate in activities that can enhance self-esteem and social skills. Teens with eating disorders long to be accepted and may look for others with eating disorders to be with so they don't feel so out of place. Having them engage with positive, accepting teens who do not have eating disorders can help enhance their self-esteem.

Put yourself in the place of teenagers: What are they reading, seeing on television, and looking at on the Internet? Watch some of the TV shows teens like and look at some of the Internet sites they are browsing. There are several dangerous Web sites that encourage eating disorders. Topics on these Web sites include tips on becoming anorexic or bulimic, low-fat and low-calorie recipes, photographs of thin celebrities, lists of reasons eating disorders are good, and pictures of emaciated women. Terms used on these sites include "thinspiration," "Ana," and "Mia." "Thinspiration" is a collection of photos of extremely thin women used to inspire people to get or stay thin. "Ana" is an abbreviation for anorexia, and "Mia" stands for bulimia. Web sites with this type of information are called Pro-Ana, Pro-Mia or Pro-Ana/Mia Web sites. Explain to the teen the destructive motivation behind these Web sites, and how they glamorize a practice that is based on self-hatred.

RESOURCES

Anorexia Nervosa and Related Eating Disorders, Inc. (anred.com).

Eating Disorder Referral and Information Center (edreferral.com).

HelpGuide.org (HelpGuide.org).

National Association of Anorexia Nervosa and Associated Disorders (anad.org). Phone: 847-831-3438.

National Eating Disorders Association (NationalEatingDisorders.org). Phone: 800-931-2237.

YoungWomensHealth.org (youngwomenshealth.org).

Eating Disorders: The Journey to Recovery Workbook by Laura Goodman and Mona Villipiano. New York: Taylor & Francis, 2000.

Weight Wisdom by K. Kingsbury and M. Williams. New York: Taylor & Francis, 2003.

NOTES

1. E. B. Gittes, "Eating Disorders in Adolescents," *Journal of Pediatric and Adolescent Gynecology* 17 (2004): 417–419.

2. National Eating Disorders Association, "Facts for Activists (or Anyone)," www.nationaleatingdisorders.org/

p.asp?WebPage_ID=320&Profile_ID=95634 (accessed September 14, 2007).

3. American Psychiatric Association Staff, *Diagnostic and Statistical Manual of Mental Disorders,* 4th ed., text revision (Washington, DC: American Psychiatric Association, 2000).

4. Helpguide.org, "Eating Disorders: Types, Warning Signs, and Treatment," www.helpguide.org/mental/ eating_disorder_treatment.htm#online (accessed September 14, 2007).

5. American Psychiatric Association Staff, *Diagnostic and Statistical Manual of Mental Disorders.*

6. Ibid.

7. Helpguide.org, "Eating Disorders."

8. American Psychiatric Association Staff, *Diagnostic and Statistical Manual of Mental Disorders.*

9. Helpguide.org, "Eating Disorders."

10. American Psychiatric Association Staff, *Diagnostic and Statistical Manual of Mental Disorders.*

What Can Teens Do about Eating Disorders?

If you are worried that you or your friend have an eating disorder, it is important to talk about it. If you don't feel comfortable talking to your friend about your worries for her, tell a trusted adult about your concerns and get help. This person could be a family member, school counselor, teacher, or some other person you trust. Talking about it could save your or your friend's life.

Things to Look For

- Obsession with weight and weight loss

- Obsession with looking thin

- Significant weight loss or gain

- Dieting when very thin

- Excessive exercise

- Obsessively counting calories and fat grams

- Constant claims of not being hungry, or finding reasons to eat excessively

- Cutting food and moving it around, but never actually eating it

- Hiding food in napkins or trash can

- Never eating in front of others

- Brittle hair and fingernails

- Wearing baggy clothing

- Unusual tooth decay and tooth loss

- Scars and redness on hands (from inducing vomiting)

- Hoarding or hiding food

- Spending excessive amounts of money on food

- Buying laxatives and diuretics (water pills)

- Depressed mood and isolation from friends

FOSTER CARE

Young people under the age of 18 are placed in foster care for numerous reasons. Youth may be placed in foster care if the courts determine that they have been abused or neglected by a parent or caregiver. In most states, law enforcement officials or physicians can place a youth in protective custody if there is imminent risk of harm to him. In some states, parents might decide to place their child in foster care through a short-term, voluntary agreement with the child welfare agency, for reasons such as being in an inpatient treatment program. Also, if a parent or someone else believes a youth's behavior is beyond the parent's control, the court can be petitioned to order services for the youth and family.[1]

Foster care is 24-hour care provided by the child welfare system for youth who need to move out of their homes temporarily. Child welfare agencies may place youth in any of the following settings: kinship care (placement with relatives), emergency shelter care, family foster care, a therapeutic foster home, a group home, a residential treatment center, or an independent living arrangement for older youth.[2] The terms "foster care" and "out-of-home placement" will be used interchangeably in this chapter.

To comply with the Adoption Assistance and Child Welfare Act of 1980, states must prepare a plan describing the efforts made to prevent removal and describing the services provided to families to facilitate reunification (a youth returning to her home). The courts play an important role in determining if continued placement with parents would be contrary to the welfare of the teen, and must later determine if continued out-of-home care is in the best interest of the youth.

In the United States, the Adoption and Safe Families Act requires states to make concerted efforts to ensure children's safety, permanency, and well-being while in foster care. This means child welfare agencies must:

1. Continually evaluate a youth's environment for safety;

2. Promote a youth's continued connection to his or her family;

3. Facilitate a stable and permanent living arrangement;

4. Take care of the youth's physical, mental, developmental, and educational needs; and

5. Provide services to the youth's family to ensure the youth's safety and well-being upon reunification (return home).

While youth are in foster care, it is the responsibility of the child welfare agency to ensure their protection.

"I didn't get any choice in being placed, but I don't know what would have happened to me if I hadn't gone." —Glen

Who Is in Foster Care?

There are over 500,000 children currently residing in foster care on almost any given day. On September 30, 2005, there were 513,000 children in the United States living in foster care. Forty-five percent were aged 12 or older, and the average length of stay in foster care was 15.5 months. A nonrelative foster home was the most common placement setting (46 percent), and the race/ethnicity of children in foster care was 41 percent White, 32 percent Black, 18 percent Latino, 3 percent biracial, 2 percent American Indian, 2 percent unknown, and 1 percent Asian American.[3]

WHAT YOU CAN DO TO HELP

Be Aware That This Is an Ever-Changing Experience

During the first few months of their placement, many youth experience a "honeymoon period" during which they are on their best behavior and are trying to figure out the new environments and expectations. They may be relieved to be out of the situation they were removed from, but anxious about what the future holds for them and their families. The youth may have changing and conflicting feelings about his parents; often, no matter how much he has been abused or neglected, he still cares about those who abused or neglected him. The roles and responsibilities the teen held in his home, no matter how degrading or unfair, were what he knew, and he may become anxious when faced with mastering new ones.

Recognize the Youth's Losses

Youth in foster care face a variety of losses when removed from their homes. A teen's losses may include her parents, community, home, school, faith community, friends, the rules and lifestyle that were her status quo, her role in her family structure, and her cultural norms. Don't minimize the amount or type of loss the teen may experience;

if she misses the person who usually bags her groceries, acknowledge this loss. Help her grieve her losses. Look at the big picture of the young person's life and accept that you don't need to know the exact questions or pains she is dealing with to be supportive; you can simply be nurturing and patient, and let her deal with things at her own pace.

If you work with a youth prior to out-of-home placement, stick with the teen and your relationship, no matter the distance. Work hard to not be counted among the youth's losses.

Acknowledge the Changes and Transitions

Along with loss comes change. Most losses the teen experiences are replaced with things over which he has no control. Almost every transition someone goes through in foster care results in a lost relationship, often replaced by a stranger: a teen can lose his teachers, the next-door neighbor, the owner of the store down the street. Even if they are being removed from negative or even dangerous influences, teens in foster care lose many significant adults and positive relationships in their lives. Most youth in foster care are living with strangers—an enormous change to adapt to. A teen may attend a new school, have multiple adults with authority over him (including child welfare workers), be adjusting to a structured life, and be living in and learning the ways of a different culture. Persistence, patience, and sincere interest are keys to developing a trusting relationship with the youth.

Respect and Support the Teen

Building a relationship based on trust and respect is the greatest gift you can give a young person who has been removed from her home. Like all youth, teens in foster care and those leaving foster care need relationships with safe, trusted adults. Youth may leave foster care and return to their homes, or "age out" of foster care at age 18, and need a person to rely on as they make these transitions. If you are unable to be that person in a teen's life, help her identify someone who can be.

Provide teens with opportunities to experience life free from abuse and neglect. Provide safe, nurturing opportunities for teens to experience their lives (their childhood) in different ways than they did at home.

You have important insight into who the youth is, how he is acting, or how he may be feeling. It is important that you report any concerns or changes, good or bad, to the custodial agency, and offer to participate in a meeting on behalf of the youth. Support the teen's participation in mental health services (if needed), educational testing, and planning services to promote the transition to independent living; these are all crucial to his future success.

And while it's important to acknowledge the enormous loss and change that comes with being in foster care, don't assume that living in foster care will be a damaging experience.

Help Teens Process Their Thoughts about Their Families of Origin

We all must abide by the parameters of the parent-child relationship as defined by the child welfare agency, which will determine such things as when, where, and how frequently family visitations can occur. In abiding by these guidelines, acknowledge that youth often want to maintain connections with their families of origin. Be open to and expect kids to talk about their families of origin. Provide teens with safe, judgment-free space to process their thoughts. Talk with them about visits they have with their families. Visitation with parents may provide teens with the opportunity to see where they fit into their families once an out-of-home placement has occurred, and to check how well they are functioning compared to their families. Be prepared to process these observations and changes with teens.

Encourage Life Skills

Youth in foster care who receive life skills preparation are more likely to achieve success in adulthood than those who do not.[4] Encourage and help teens connect to life skills courses. Find out if your agency or program can add life skills preparation to your programming. Life skills training can include teaching skills related to career planning, communication, daily living, home life, housing

and money management, self-care, social relationships, work life, and work and study skills. Is your agency/program a natural match to any of these? What are small ways you could incorporate life skills preparation into what you're already doing? Customized learning plans with a clear outline and accompanying teaching resources are available for free or at a minimal cost at caseylifeskills.org.

This chapter includes writings from contributing author Heather M. Pautz

"Before I got put into foster care I was always getting into a lot of trouble. I was scared to get placed—I didn't want to go, I wanted to stay with my dad, for me it was scary. I was about 16 when it happened and I had heard all this stuff about foster homes that scared me. I know foster care is different for everyone and not everyone will get foster parents like I did, but foster care ended up being a good thing. It was easy for me in their home because being there helped me a lot, I quit doing drugs, I quit hanging around all the people that were bad influences. I started to do a lot more thinking, I was able to grow up a lot when I was with them. I had goals, which I had never had before." —Glen

RESOURCES

Administration for Children and Families (acf.hhs.gov).

FosterClub, The National Network for Children and Youth in Foster Care (fosterclub.com).

The National Network for Foster Children and Foster Youth (fyi3.com).

SAFY Specialized Alternatives for Families and Youth (safy.org).

Beyond the Foster Care System: The Future for Teens by Betsy Krebs and Paul Pitcoff. New Brunswick, NJ: Rutgers University Press, 2006.

A House Between Homes: Youth in the Foster Care System by Joyce Libal. Broomall, PA: Mason Crest Publishers, 2004.

Stay Close: 40 Clever Ways to Connect with Kids When You're Apart by Tenessa Gemelke. Minneapolis: Search Institute, 2005.

Working with Traumatized Youth in Child Welfare (Social Work Practice with Children and Families), edited by Nancy Boyd Webb. New York: Guilford Press, 2006.

Youth Who Chronically AWOL from Foster Care: Why They Run, Where They Go, and What Can Be Done by Marni Finklestein, Mark Wamsley, Dan Currie, and Dorenne Miranda. New York: Vera Institute of Justice, 2004.

NOTES

1. J. McCarthy, A. Marshal, J. Collins, G. Arganza, K. Deserly, and J. Milon, *A Family's Guide to the Child Welfare System* (Washington, DC: Collaborative effort among National Technical Assistance Center for Children's Mental Health at Georgetown University Center for Child and Human Development, Technical Assistance Partnership for Child and Family Mental Health at American Institutes for Research, Federation of Families for Children's Mental Health, Child Welfare League of America, and National Indian Welfare Association, 2003).

2. Ibid.

3. U.S. Department of Health and Human Services, "The Adoption and Foster Care Analysis and Reporting System Report, 2006," www.acf.hhs.gov/programs/cb/stats_research/afcars/tar/report11.htm (accessed September 24, 2007).

4. Foster Care Alumni Studies, *Assessing the Effects of Foster Care: Early Results from the Casey National Alumni Study* (Seattle, WA: Casey Family Programs, 2003), p. 3.

How You Can Help Kids in Foster Care

Be aware that foster care is an ever-changing experience. The roles and responsibilities the youth held in his home, no matter how degrading or unfair, were what he knew, and he may become anxious when faced with a new role and new responsibilities.

Recognize the youth's losses. A teen's losses may include her parents, her community, her home, her school, her faith community, her friends, the rules and lifestyle that were her status quo, her role in their family structure, her cultural norms. Never minimize the amount or type of loss the teen may experience. Help her grieve her losses.

Respect and support the teen. Building a relationship based on trust and respect is the greatest gift you can give a youth who has been removed from his home. Like all youth, teens in foster care and those leaving foster care need relationships with safe, trusted adults.

Avoid demonizing foster care. While we must acknowledge the enormous loss and changes that come with being in foster care, we should not assume that living in foster care will be a damaging experience.

Help teens process their thoughts about their families of origin. Be open to and expect kids to talk about their families of origin. Provide teens with safe, judgment-free space to process their thoughts.

Encourage life skills. Encourage and help teens connect to life skills courses. Find out if your agency or program can add life skills preparation to its programming.

GANGS

Gangs are groups of teens and young adults who typically carry out illegal and violent acts. They are a problem in cities, rural areas, and suburban areas. Kids and teens of all ethnicities and income levels are at risk for being involved in a gang. Gang members usually claim an area of town as their turf, and challenge rival gang members to maintain their space. Gang members may have tattoos symbolizing their affiliation, and they may have nicknames for each other. Once in a gang, a person must adhere to the strict gang code of conduct or risk a beating, or even death. Many teens are forced to join gangs for their own protection, but some teens join a gang because they want to feel a sense of belonging.

Gang life can be extremely dangerous. When a boy joins a gang, he may be "beat in" and forced to fight several other gang members at once. When a girl joins a gang, she may be required to have sex with several gang members as part of her initiation, or she may be forced to fight several other girl members of the gang. Other initiation activities might include committing crimes—even robbing or killing someone. Once in a gang, members may be required to commit crimes, and many gang members end up in jail.

Gang Members and Gang Trends

According to the National Gang Crime Research Center, gang members are more likely to have been bullies in school, and they report having had less-than-adequate parental supervision when they were children. Gang members are also more likely to come from a mother-only home.[1]

The National Gang Crime Research Center also reported that slightly more than half of the gang members surveyed were recruited to be in a gang, and just under half volunteered to join a gang—and about a third have successfully hidden their gang involvement from their parents. Once youth are in a gang, about half of those surveyed have committed a crime. They are more likely to put themselves in situations that may risk personal injury, and more likely to report that they have shot a gun at a police officer. About half of gang members have tried to quit gang life, and almost 80 percent of gang members surveyed stated they would quit their gang if given a new start in life.[2]

Gangs in the Community

Gang membership carries many negative consequences for an individual, but it also results in systemic problems for the community or school. Gangs engage in prolific acts of vandalism, including graffiti. Graffiti may appear on school buildings or other public property, but can also be on a teen's personal belongings and his school books. Because many gangs are involved in drug dealing, the presence of a gang in the community can lead to the presence of drugs, guns, and other dangerous items on or near school property. Gang members (especially older members) may loiter on or near school property if other gang members are attending school. This can pose a danger to other students in the school. When gangs are present, there may be an increase in fighting and other types of violence, placing many people at risk of injury, or even death. Gang activity in a school can create a culture of fear, intimidation, and bullying.

Why Do Teens Join Gangs?

One might wonder why anyone would want to join a gang. Often, teens join to feel that they belong. They might feel that their gang is like a family, and find comfort in being part of a group they can identify with, and from whom they can receive protection. Teens in a gang may also feel a sense of power because others fear the members of their gang. Sometimes teens join gangs for the perceived prestige; they may be lured into joining with promises of clothes, shoes, or other expensive items that teens value. Once someone is in a gang, it is difficult or impossible to leave it. Preventing teens from joining a gang is the best way to deal with the problem of gangs.

Some Signs That a Teen Is Involved in a Gang

Telltale signs that a teen may be involved in a gang include the clothing the young person wears. Clothing indicators can include wearing one color excessively or exclusively, wearing baggy pants, wearing jewelry only on one side of the body, or wearing pant legs or collars in certain ways. However, some clothing styles associated with gangs are now popular among many teens, so look for other signs in addition to clothing. Gang members may give each other particular hand signals or handshakes, draw graffiti-like gang symbols, or use odd-sounding language. More general behavior problems may also suggest involvement in a gang. These include trouble in school, withdrawing from family, drinking or doing drugs, and getting in legal trouble. Other signs may be unexplained injuries, excessive cash or expensive possessions, and hanging out with friends who also display many of these signs. The greater the number of signs a teen displays, the more likely she is involved in a gang—but any one of these signs alone doesn't necessarily mean a teen is in a gang.

WHAT YOU CAN DO TO HELP

Educate Yourself

There are things you can do as an individual to help teens who are in a gang, or who are at risk for being in a gang. Obtain education about the particular gangs in your community. Having knowledge of the colors, type of graffiti, and behaviors of local gang members can help you identify gang behavior and report it to authorities. Knowing what to look for can also help you intervene early with a teen you suspect is a gang member. If you think a teen is in a gang, set him up with a positive peer or mentor so that he develops a positive relationship with someone who is not in a gang. You can also refer a gang member for counseling, or start a support group for teens who are in a gang and want to get out. It may be best to approach him when he is alone, and not in front of other gang members. It is important to remember that even though he may be in a gang, he is still not an adult and may need someone who will reach out to him and let him know he is cared for.

Work with the Community

Many gang awareness and gang prevention programs are available for schools or communities to implement. Education about gangs can help a community build immunity to the problems that gangs cause. Community members can work together to remove graffiti and report suspicious activities. Neighborhood watches can help curb gang behaviors and increase neighborhood cohesiveness. Extra security measures can be employed to make schools safer against gang and other types of violence.

Focus on Prevention

With gangs, prevention is the best intervention. As a parent or guardian, you can increase family activities and involvement with your kids. It is important to set clear guidelines and expectations about what behaviors are acceptable and what are not. Spending family time together might decrease the chances that a teen will feel the need to join a gang. Encourage kids and teens to be involved in sports or other positive activities, and provide a positive adult role model for teens. Educating kids and teens about gangs and the dangers of gangs can help them make better choices if they are approached by gang members.

Gangs can cause many problems for teens, and sometimes intervening with teens may be starting too late. Gangs are recruiting members at a very young age. Implementing gang prevention programs with younger kids is key to curbing a gang problem.

RESOURCES

Gang Prevention Network (gangprevention.org). Information and resources about gangs and gang prevention.

Gang Reduction through Intervention, Prevention and Education (GRIPE) (gripe4rkids.org).

National Gang Research Center (ngcrc.com).

Robert Walker's Gangs or Us (gangsorus.com).

An Introduction to Gangs by George W. Knox. Peotone, IL: New Chicago School Press, 2006.

Teen Gangs: A Global View, edited by Maureen P. Duffy and Scott Edward Gillig. Westport, CT: Greenwood Press, 2004.

NOTES

1. George W. Knox et al., *The Facts about Gang Life in America Today: A National Study of over 4,000 Gang Members* (National Gang Crime Research Center, 1997), www.ngcrc.com/ngcrc/page9.htm (accessed November 2, 2007).

2. Ibid.

Signs of Gang Involvement

- Wearing one particular color of clothing excessively or exclusively

- Wearing baggy pants

- Tattoos or temporary tattoos that signify gang membership or wanting to be in a gang

- Using hand signals to communicate with friends

- Graffiti-like writing on belongings

- Withdrawing from family and positive friends

- Using drugs or alcohol

- Having unexplained amounts of cash or new expensive possessions

- Having unexplained injuries or lying about the causes of injuries

- Defying adults, being in legal trouble

- Hanging out with friends who display many of these signs

Dealing with Gangs and Preventing Gang Membership

- Educate yourself and teens about gangs: the more teens know about the negative consequences of gangs, the less likely they will be to join.

- Involve teens in positive activities, such as sports.

- Spend quality family time together.

- Reach out and engage a troubled kid in a mentoring relationship.

- Organize a neighborhood watch and report gang activity.

- Set clear rules and expectations about being involved in a gang. Be clear that gang activity is not acceptable.

Reprinted with permission from *Helping Teens Handle Tough Experiences: Strategies to Foster Resilience*, by Jill Nelson and Sarah Kjos. Copyright © 2008 by Search Institute®, Minneapolis, Minnesota, 800-888-7828, www.search-institute.org. All rights reserved.

GAY, LESBIAN, BISEXUAL, TRANSGENDER, OR QUESTIONING TEENS

Being gay, lesbian, bisexual, transgender, or questioning one's sexual orientation and/or gender identity (GLBTQ) is not in and of itself an adversity—rather, being GLBTQ in a society that has historically disapproved of these lifestyles can bring significant difficulties. This chapter provides a brief overview of issues specific to the GLBTQ population, focusing primarily on education, as knowledge on these issues can be your most powerful aid in becoming an ally to GLBTQ youth.

Who Are GLBTQ?

People who are GLBTQ are sometimes called the "invisible minority." While the precise number of people who are gay, lesbian, or bisexual is unknown, it is generally agreed that at least 10 percent of our population is GLB. It is difficult to determine the prevalence of transgender people accurately, but current estimates of transsexualism are about 1 in 10,000 for biological males and 1 in 30,000 for biological females; the number of people in other transgender categories is unknown.[1] Regardless of how percentages and numbers are derived, people who come under the GLBTQ umbrella constitute a significant minority group. You have worked with people who are gay, lesbian, bisexual, transgender, or questioning, regardless of whether they are "out" to you or others.

Homophobia and Heterosexism

Homophobia and heterosexism are at the heart of why being GLBTQ can be a difficult experience.

Homophobia is the irrational fear of, disgust with, or hatred toward gays, lesbians, or bisexuals, or of homosexual feelings in oneself. Homophobia refers to the discomfort one feels with any behavior, belief, or attitude that does not conform to traditional sex role stereotypes. Homophobia results in negative behaviors toward and fears of gay, lesbian, and bisexual people. Heterosexism is a form of oppression that targets gays, lesbians, and bisexuals, and includes beliefs about the superiority of heterosexuality and the inferiority of homosexuality, as well as the assigning of rights and privileges to heterosexuals that are denied to gay, lesbian, and bisexual people.

WHAT YOU CAN DO TO HELP

Understand the Distinction between Sexual Orientation and Gender Identity

Sexual orientation and gender identity are different. *Sexual orientation* describes which sex(es) you are attracted to; heterosexuals are attracted to the opposite sex, homosexuals are attracted to the same sex, and bisexuals are attracted to both sexes. *Gender identity* is how you see yourself: as male, female, or a combination of both. Gender identity may or may not be the same as your biological sex. There is a continuum of gender, which isn't always easily categorized: there are more terms and descriptors for gender identity than simply "male" or "female" (one person described her gender as "the gender between my ears," meaning she knows she is female regardless of her anatomy). Gender identity often evolves early in life.

> "When I was 5 years old I would tell my mom I was a boy. I was met with complete anger and resistance. It was the only time I would hear my mom yell. Her own lack of knowledge and fear hurt me. I had stereotypes pushed on me, due to binary logic. Since I've transitioned, I still have people who insist on calling me by my old name and by female pronouns."
> —Andrew

It is important not to assume that sexual orientation and gender identity go hand in hand. For example, because a man is gay does not mean he wants to be a woman. Most people who are gay or lesbian do not want to change their sex. While some people who are gay, lesbian, bisexual, or straight dress and behave in ways outside of our gender-role stereotypes (for example, girls wearing clothing that we as a society have determined are "boy's clothes"), it does not mean they want to be the opposite sex.

Learn the Language

Become familiar with common terms used to define gender identity. The following terms do not constitute a comprehensive list of the many forms of gender identity, but they do provide a starting point for understanding. You'll be more equipped to talk with teens about sexual orientation and gender identity when you have an understanding of the common vocabulary. The more common definitions, as written by Outfront Minnesota, include:

Bisexual: A person who experiences the human need for warmth, affection, and love from persons of either gender. Sometimes this includes sexual contact.

Gay: A man (or boy) who experiences the human need for warmth, affection, and love from other men. This term is also used to apply to both men and women who are attracted to the same gender.

Lesbian: A woman (or girl) who experiences the human need for warmth, affection, and love from other women. Sometimes this includes sexual contact.

Transgender: An umbrella term for persons who have a self-image or gender identity not traditionally associated with their biological gender. Some transgender persons wish to change their anatomy to be more congruent with their self-perception, while others do not have such a desire.

Transsexual: A person whose gender identity is other than their biological gender; most transsexuals would like to alter their bodies to be congruent with their self-perception.

> "I was 4 years old when I knew dresses weren't my gig. I looked like a little boy, my clothes, my haircuts, and even though I was mistaken as a boy, I didn't want to be one. Other people were uncomfortable, but I was so perfectly comfortable, I had pride about being a girl." —Jade

Cross-dressers: A person who dresses in the clothing of the opposite biological gender. They generally want to be related to, and be accepted as, a person of the gender they are presenting.

Intersexed (once called hermaphrodites): Generally applied to individuals born with ambiguous genitalia.[2]

Understand the Impact of Homophobia and Heterosexism on Adolescents

Homophobia and heterosexism interfere with the developmental tasks typical of adolescent development. Adolescence involves physical, cognitive, and psychosocial development. It is developmentally appropriate for teens to seek answers to questions about their identity, integrity, attraction, and independence. GLBTQ youth are seeking answers about their sexual orientation and/or gender identity in a society that doesn't always value the answer when it is "I am GLBTQ." A GLBTQ youth trying to answer the question, "Who am I?" is seeking answers to her identity development in a culture filled with derogatory images and commentary about an integral part of who she is. This can lead to feeling devalued and possibly to pretending to be heterosexual in order to be accepted. Acceptance based on deception can make teens feel further isolated from others and the community.

This is a very brief overview of the impact of homophobia and heterosexism on GLBTQ youth:

- After coming out to their families, or being discovered, many GLBTQ youth are thrown out of their homes, mistreated, or made the focus of their families' dysfunction.[3]

- Youth of color are significantly less likely to have told their parent(s) they are GLBTQ; one study found that while 80 percent of GLBTQ Whites were out to their parent(s), only 71 percent of Latinos, 61 percent of African Americans, and 51 percent of Asian Americans and Pacific Islanders were out to their parent(s).[4]

- In one national survey, almost two-thirds of GLBT youth reported that they felt unsafe in their schools because of their sexual orientation, and over one-third reported they felt unsafe because of their gender expression. Over a third of students reported at least some experience of physical harassment because of their sexual

orientation, and nearly 20 percent of youth reported some incident of physical assault in the past year due to their sexual orientation; over 10 percent reported having been assaulted because of their gender expression.[5]

- The consequences of physical and verbal abuse directed at GLBTQ students include truancy, dropping out of school, poor grades, and having to repeat a grade. In one study, 28 percent of gay and bisexual youth dropped out of school due to peer harassment.[6]

- GLBTQ youth who use drugs and alcohol may do so for many of the same reasons as heterosexuals, but their vulnerability is enhanced by social isolation and the need to hide sexual orientation; substance abuse may be motivated by the attempt to manage stigma and shame, to deny same-sex feelings, or to defend against ridicule and anti-gay violence.[7]

- In a recent survey, 25 percent of gay, lesbian, and bisexual high school students reported attempting suicide in the previous year, compared to 6 percent of their heterosexual peers.[8]

Use Neutral Language and GLBTQ-Friendly Symbolism

Neutral language makes no assumptions about sexual orientation. For example, if you're talking to a teen boy, avoid questions like, "So, do you have a girlfriend?" These questions, even when asked in the context of attempting to better understand a youth's life, can throw up a brick wall for GLBTQ youth. It is also important to steer away from assumptions about relationships, partners, or attraction, even when you know the teen has previously been in a heterosexual relationship, as some teens are questioning or are bisexual.

If your program uses registration forms that caregivers must fill out, eliminate "Mom/Dad" language, both because not all children live with their parents and because some teens have same-sex parents. Simply replacing "Mom/Dad" with "Guardian(s)" acknowledges that families are composed in many ways.

Using symbolism indicates to youth who are aware of the symbols that you are a person they can trust. The best-known symbols of gay allies are a rainbow flag and a pink triangle in a green circle, the "safe-zone symbol." Having a rainbow flag or safe-zone symbol in your office space can lead to conversations with kids who are curious about what the symbols mean. It is important to acknowledge that displaying GLBTQ allied symbols in the workplace may be easier if you are a heterosexual ally, since people who are GLBTQ may not want to "come out" in the workplace.

Take a Stand against Homophobic Language

It's hard to imagine that anyone who has worked with teens hasn't heard "that's so gay" or similar statements. These comments are made so frequently by teens (and adults) and often so overlooked by adults that they become a "normal" part of language and teen culture. When countering negative remarks, open up the conversation to the teen rather than simply saying, "That's not ok." Give the teen time to process the reasons why a comment is unacceptable. Have these conversations with teens (and adults) frequently and give each conversation time for both of you to think.

When a Teen Is Directly Faced with Homophobia or Heterosexism

Employ your GLBTQ-friendly language and knowledge while empathically listening to a teen share what he is experiencing. If a teen has been threatened or verbally abused, check the policy and procedures guidelines for the environment in which the event took place (such as in a school). If there is a violation of policy and a grievance procedure, let the teen know he has the choice to pursue the issue. Be aware of how difficult this choice may be for a teen, as it may mean outing himself, retaliation, or ridicule. Let the teen know he has a right to a safe environment and protection, even if an agency or entity fails to provide it. Remind GLBTQ youth that these incidents are not their fault, but the result of a lack of care and understanding. Your support and understanding can help GLBTQ youth feel more comfortable being part of your program or agency. Encourage them to continue to come forward with the challenges they face.

RESOURCES

GTR: Gay Teen Resources (gayteens.org). The oldest, largest, and established online LGBT international youth site.

NYAC: National Youth Advocacy Coalition (nyacyouth.org). Phone: 800-541-6922. Social justice organization that advocates for and with young people who are LGBTQ in an effort to end discrimination against these youth and to ensure their physical and emotional well-being.

The Trevor Project: Saving Young Lives (thetrevorproject.org). Phone: 866-4-U-TREVOR. The Trevor Project is dedicated to educating people about gay and questioning youth and providing a crisis and suicide hotline for gay and questioning youth.

Youth Resource (youthresource.com). A Web site by and for GLBTQ young people that takes a holistic approach to sexual health and exploring issues of concern to GLBTQ youth.

Am I Blue? Coming Out from the Silence, edited by Marion Dane Bauer. New York: HarperCollins, 1994.

Coming Out of the Classroom Closet: Gay and Lesbian Students, Teachers, and Curricula, edited by Karen M. Harbeck. New York: Haworth Press, 1992.

GLBTQ: The Survival Guide for Queer and Questioning Teens by Kelly Huegel. Minneapolis: Free Spirit Publishing, 2003.

Growing Up Gay: The Sorrows and Joys of Gay and Lesbian Adolescence by Rita Reed. New York: W. W. Norton & Company, 1997.

Growing Up Gay in America: Informative and Practical Advice for Teen Guys Questioning Their Sexuality and Growing Up Gay by Jason R. Rich. Portland, OR: Franklin Street Books, 2002.

School Experiences of Gay and Lesbian Youth: The Invisible Minority, edited by Mary B. Harris. New York: Harrington Park Press, 1997.

Sexual Orientation and School Policy: A Practical Guide for Teachers, Administrators, and Community Activists by Ian K. Macgillivray. Lanham, MD: Rowman & Littlefield, 2004.

NOTES

1. American Psychological Association Task Force on Gender Identity, Gender Variance, and Intersex Conditions, M. Schneider et al., *Answers to Your Questions about Transgender Individuals and Gender Identity*, 2007, www.apa.org/topics/transgender.html (accessed September 24, 2007).

2. Outfront Minnesota, "Definitions: Terms Commonly Associated with the Gay, Lesbian, Bisexual, and Transgender Communities," www.outfront.org/library/definitions.html (accessed January 18, 2008).

3. R. C. Savin-Williams, "Verbal and Physical Abuse as Stressors in the Lives of Lesbian, Gay Male, and Bisexual Youths: Associates with School Problems, Runaway, Substance Abuse, Prostitution, and Suicide," *Journal of Consulting and Clinical Psychology* 62 (1994): 261–269.

4. C. Grov and D. S. Bimbi, "Race, Ethnicity, Gender, and Generational Factors Associated with the Coming Out Process among Gay, Lesbian, and Bisexual Individuals," *Journal of Sex Research* 43 (2006): 115–121.

5. J. G. Kosciw, *The 2003 National School Climate Survey: The School-Related Experiences of Our Nation's Lesbian, Gay, Bisexual and Transgender Youth* (New York: Gay, Lesbian and Straight Education Network, 2004), 29–31.

6. Savin-Williams, "Verbal and Physical Abuse as Stressors."

7. C. Ryan and D. Futterman, *Lesbian and Gay Youth: Care and Counseling* (New York: Columbia University Press, 1998), 45.

8. Massachusetts Department of Education, (2005). "Massachusetts high school students and sexual orientation: results of the 2005 youth risk behavior survey." www.mass.gov/cgly/yrbs05.pdf (accessed September 24, 2007).

How to Start a Gay-Straight Alliance

1. Follow Guidelines

Establish a GSA the same way you would establish any other group or club. Look in your Student Handbook for your school's rules. This may include getting permission from an administrator or writing a constitution.

2. Find a Faculty Advisor

Find a teacher or staff member who you think would be supportive or who has already shown themselves to be an ally around sexual orientation issues. It could be a teacher, counselor, nurse, or librarian.

3. Inform Administration of Your Plans

Tell administrators what you are doing right away. It can be very helpful to have them on your side. They can work as liaisons to teachers, parents, community members, and the school board. If an administrator opposes the GSA, inform them that forming a GSA club is protected under the Federal Equal Access Act.

4. Inform Guidance Counselors and Social Workers about the Group

These individuals may know students who would be interested in attending the group.

5. Pick a Meeting Place

You may want to find a meeting place that is off the beaten track at school and offers some level of privacy.

6. Advertise

Figure out the best way to advertise at your school. It may be a combination of your school bulletin, flyers, and word of mouth. If your flyers are defaced or torn down, do not be discouraged. Keep putting them back up. Eventually, whoever is tearing them down will give up. Besides, advertising your group and having words up such as "gay lesbian, bisexual, transgender, or questioning" or "end homophobia" can be part of educating the school and can actually make other students feel safer—even if they never attend a single meeting.

7. Get Food

This one is kind of obvious. People always come to meetings when you provide food!

8. Hold Your Meeting!

You may want to start out with a discussion about why people feel having this group is important. You can also brainstorm things your club would like to do this year.

9. Establish Ground Rules

Many groups have ground rules in order to insure that group discussions are safe, confidential, and respectful. Many groups have a ground rule that no assumptions or labels are used about a group member's sexual orientation. This can help make straight allies feel comfortable about attending the club.

10. Plan for the Future

Develop an action plan. Brainstorm activities. Set goals for what you want to work toward. Contact Gay-Straight Alliance Network in order to get connected to other GSAs, get supported, and learn about what else is going on in the community.

For more information and resources for Gay-Straight Alliance, contact GSA Network: Statewide Office: 1550 Bryant Street #800, San Francisco, CA 94103, phone: 415-552-4229, fax: 415-552-4729 • Central Valley Office: 928 N. Van Ness Ave., Fresno, CA 93728, phone: 559-266-2780, fax: 559-266-2766 • Southern California Office: 605 W. Olympic Blvd., Suite 610, Los Angeles, CA 90015, phone: 213-534-7162, fax: 213-553-1833 • www.gsanetwork.org

HOMELESSNESS

Adults, children, and families are homeless for myriad reasons. The broad factors contributing to homelessness are poverty, eroding work opportunities, a decline in public assistance, a lack of affordable housing and limited housing assistance programs, lack of affordable health care, domestic violence, mental illness, and addiction disorders.[1]

A homeless teen may be sleeping in a car in a parking lot, staying on a friend's couch, temporarily staying in a hotel, living in a tent, or living in precarious housing. Families may be living in similar situations, or in a shelter, or be "doubled up" with other families in a small space (a hotel room, efficiency apartment, or relative's home).

Who Are Homeless Youth?

Some homeless teens are part of a homeless family, while others have left home on their own as a result of physical and/or sexual abuse, strained relationships, chemical addiction of a family member, or parental neglect. Independent, homeless teens, often referred to as unaccompanied youth, are individuals under the age of 18 who lack parental, foster, or institutional care.[2] Estimates of the homeless youth population range from 52,000 to over 1 million, while estimates of runaways, including "throwaway" youth, are between 1 million and 1.7 million.[3]

WHAT YOU CAN DO TO HELP

Learn the Various Definitions of "Homelessness"

Definitions of homelessness vary from program to program. It is helpful and time efficient when working with teens (especially those you may have very limited time with) to know which programs you have in your area for homeless youth and what specifically qualifies participants as "homeless." Homelessness can range from living on the street to living in a wide range of temporary situations. Becoming aware of the many varied definitions, and the specific definition each of your local programs adheres to, can help in connecting children and families to services they need.

Learn the Educational Rights of Homeless Youth

One of our greatest tools in assisting homeless youth is connecting them with the services they, by law, have access to in every public school district in the United States. The McKinney-Vento Homeless Assistance Act of 1987 (Subtitle B-Education for Homeless Children and Youth), renewed in January 2002, ensures educational rights and protections for homeless school-aged youth.

Becoming familiar with this act can assist you in advocating for the educational rights of youth with whom you may work. Under the McKinney-Vento Act, children who are homeless have the right to go to school no matter where they live and, if reasonable, maintain their enrollment at the school they attended prior to becoming homeless. Other provisions under this act give homeless youth the right to free or reduced-cost school meals, and immediate enrollment in school regardless of whether the youth has documents the school requires (e.g., immunization records and prior school records).

Every school district in the United States is mandated to have a liaison for homeless children whose job is to ensure access to school services for these youth. You can find out who the liaison is in your school district(s) by contacting your school district's administrative office. The handout in this chapter gives an overview of the services all homeless students are entitled to receive through their school district. Include the name and contact information of the homeless liaison when giving families this handout. Check to see if your school district has posters describing their homeless services that you can display in your program or facility.

Identify Who Is Homeless

Identification is one of the most important roles we can play in assisting homeless youth. Identifying homeless youth can help connect them to the best services and ensure that they know their educational rights. Be aware that a teen may be homeless regardless of how she is dressed or whether she provides an address, and seek to learn more about her, such as her home life, basic needs, and the barriers she faces. Asking basic, nonconfrontational questions about a teen's living situation may generate a conversation about her housing. Simply by being more aware of the possibility that someone may be homeless, you'll be more likely to learn whether a youth is in fact experiencing homelessness, and you can become her ally more quickly.

It is common for homeless youth and families to lack documentation (IDs, Social Security cards, birth certificates), attend numerous schools, and be guarded in their disclosure of being homeless. This guardedness may be due to a variety of reasons, including embarrassment, as they may be fearful of judgment from both adults and peers; fear of being removed from the place where they currently reside (consider those who fled their homes due to sexual abuse and now fear that disclosure will lead to their being returned to the abusive situation); or worry that if they disclose their homeless situation, then their parent(s) and living situation will be monitored by authorities. If you suspect a youth or family is homeless, open the door to disclosure by clarifying the roles you can and cannot play in assisting the family.

> "People need to think about the definition of homeless and what it means to be homeless. I couch surfed, so I had a roof over my head, but my car was my address. I was in some precarious situations when I would stay with other people, but I did what I had to do to survive." —Melanie

Consider the Teen's Living Conditions

Homeless people often live in crowded, substandard situations that may lack access to shower, laundry, and kitchen facilities. Imagine living in a situation like this: sleeping in a small room with many other people, lacking a refrigerator to store milk for your breakfast, lacking privacy to get ready for the day, and doing your homework while worrying if you'll still be able to stay there that night. Working from a strength-based approach with homeless youth includes acknowledging the stress, anxiety, and difficulties they experience, while honoring their coping skills and courage.

Help Obtain Documentation

Many of us grow up having a safe and secure place to store the documents we will need throughout life, such as our birth certificate and Social Security card. Many of us can name the medical providers we've seen and have a permanent place to store our medical records, including immunizations. Many of us can easily list the schools we've attended in our lives. Homeless youth likely have a very different experience.

Many homeless youth lack any official documentation, and are unsure where their last school records would be found. To compound this difficulty, youth may not have an address where documents can be sent. Knowing which agencies can assist with obtaining documents, and seeing if your program or agency can help a teen purchase a copy of her birth certificate, for example, can be enormously useful. Documentation is necessary for many services, jobs, and housing programs; helping families and youth obtain documents can open the doors to more opportunities for self-sufficiency.

Provide Basic Necessities

Is it possible for your agency, program, or site to provide basic necessities for homeless youth? Making supplies readily available for the taking, no strings attached, gives youth the things they need without having to disclose that they are in need. Basic supplies may be too expensive for teens living on few resources. Ideas to discuss and implement include the following:

- Make available hygiene bags that include deodorant, a toothbrush, toothpaste, shampoo, soap, combs, tampons, and tissues for kids to grab. If possible, provide these supplies in a sturdy backpack.

- If your site has laundry facilities, is it possible to open up their use to youth? If not, could your program provide gift certificates to a Laundromat?

- Could your program/site have juice boxes, trail mix, and other nonperishable, healthy foods readily available?

- If you are involved with a program that requires uniforms or field trip fees, for example, how can your program set aside funds to assist youth unable to afford these expenses so they

can participate in your activities? How can you publicize the fact that you will include all youth regardless of financial ability?

- Can your program/site work with youth regardless of the documentation they are able to provide? What is the minimum amount of documentation you could require to eliminate barriers to your program?

RESOURCES

National Center for Homeless Education (serve.org/nche). This site includes contact information for each State Coordinator for Homeless Education.

National Coalition for the Homeless (nationalhomeless.org).

National Network for Youth (NN4Youth.org).

National Runaway Switchboard (1800runaway.org). A 24-hour crisis line. Phone: 800-RUNAWAY.

Street Kids International (streetkids.org). A Canadian nonprofit agency founded in 1988 that develops locally relevant workshops to engage youth.

Beyond the Shelter Wall: Homeless Families Speak Out by Ralph da Costa Nunez. New York: White Tiger Press, 2004.

Our Runaway and Homeless Youth: A Guide to Understanding by Natasha Slesnick. Westport, CT: Praeger, 2004.

Out of Sight, Out of Mind: Homeless Children and Families in Small-Town America by Yvonne M. Vissing. Lexington, KY: University Press of Kentucky, 1996.

A Shelter Is Not a Home—Or Is It? Lessons from Family Homelessness in New York City by Ralph da Costa Nunez. New York: White Tiger Press, 2004.

NOTES

1. National Coalition for the Homeless, "Why Are People Homeless?" 2006, www.nationalhomeless.org/publications/facts.html (accessed May 30, 2007).

2. National Coalition for the Homeless, "Homeless Youth," 2006, www.nationalhomeless.org/publications/facts.html (accessed May 30, 2007).

3. Adrienne L. Fernandez, "*Runaway and Homeless Youth: Demographics, Programs, and Emerging issues,*" Congressional Research Service Report for Congress, www.endhomelessness.org/content/article/detail/1451 (accessed December 10, 2007).

The Educational Rights of Homeless Youth

Name and contact info of District Homeless Liaison: _____

If your family lives in any of the following situations:

In a shelter, motel, vehicle, or campground;

On the street;

In an abandoned building, trailer, or other inadequate accommodations; or

Doubled up with friends or relatives because you cannot find or afford housing;

you have certain rights or protections under the McKinney-Vento Homeless Education Assistance Act. You have the right to:

- Go to school, no matter where you live or how long you have lived there. You must be given access to the same public education provided to other students.

- Continue in the school you attended before you became homeless, or the school you last attended, if that is your choice and is feasible. The school district's local liaison for homeless education must assist you, if needed, and offer you the right to appeal a decision regarding your choice of school if it goes against your wishes.

- Receive transportation to the school you attended before you became homeless, or the school you last attended, if you request such transportation.

- Attend a school and participate in school programs with students who are not homeless. Students cannot be separated from the regular school program because they are homeless.

- Enroll in a school without giving a permanent address. Schools cannot require proof of residency that might prevent or delay school enrollment.

- Enroll and attend classes while the school arranges for the transfer of school and immunization records or any other documents required for enrollment.

- Enroll and attend classes in the school of your choice even while you and the school seek to resolve a dispute over enrollment.

- Receive the same special programs and services, if needed, as provided to all other students served in these programs.

- Receive transportation to school and to school programs.

When you move, you should do the following:

- Contact the school district's local liaison for homeless education for help with enrolling in a new school or arranging to continue in your former school.

- Tell your teachers anything that you think they need to know to help you in school.

- Ask the local liaison for homeless education, the shelter provider, or social worker for assistance with clothing and supplies, if needed.

If you need further assistance, call the National Center for Homeless Education at the toll-free helpline number: 800-308-2145

MENTALLY ILL PARENTS OR CAREGIVERS

There are numerous challenges that parents and caregivers face. When parents or caregivers have a mental illness, these challenges increase—and sometimes have a negative effect on the children they are raising. Teens who have parents or guardians with a mental illness often are more vulnerable to psychosocial and environmental risks than their peers are. How the person with the mental illness manages his symptoms, the severity of the illness, and the resulting familial stressors all play a role in how much risk children will endure.

"It was really hard growing up with a dad with schizophrenia. We never knew what to expect, especially if he wasn't on his meds. He could be really mean and abusive to all of us. Even though I am an adult and don't rely on him for support I worry about him. I don't have regular contact with him and have heard that he has been homeless at times. I also worry that I might get schizophrenia—that part worries me the most." —Ryan

As an adult, living with a mental illness is difficult. If you know a youth whose parent is living with a mental illness, try to learn as much as you can about the specific illness involved, and ways in which the results of a parent's illness might manifest in a teen's life.

Who Suffers from Mental Illness?

There are no national data on how often adults with mental illness bear and care for children, but there are likely millions of people who fall into this category.[1] The majority of American adults are parents, and as many as five million adults are diagnosed with a severe mental illness each year, so there is a very good chance that there are millions of parents with a mental illness who are caring for children. Many of the parents with a mental illness receive mental health services, and there are some steps built into the system for inquiries about their children. There is no way to know how many parents and guardians caring for children have an undiagnosed mental illness or are not receiving services.

What Risks Do Teens Face?

Children of biological parents with a mental illness have an increased risk of being diagnosed with a mental illness and are at risk for having emotional and behavior problems.[2] Biology and genetics play a role in many of the increased risk factors teens face, but they are certainly not the only factors (nor does that mean that a youth whose parent has a mental illness is destined to have problems). There are several other risk factors for children whose parents or guardians live with a mental illness.

Children and teens of parents or caregivers with a mental illness are at a greater risk for poverty, being in a single-parent family, and having poor communication with their parents or guardians. Their parents or guardians are also more likely to be aggressive or hostile, have a substance-abuse disorder, and have occupational problems.[3]

The degree to which a person's symptoms interfere with his ability to function in daily life will often put him and his children at a greater risk for unemployment and poverty. Sometimes a mental illness will cause a person to lose a job, or force him to be underemployed because he is no longer able to work at the same income level. Depending on the severity of the symptoms, a person with a mental illness may be on disability, leaving him with a steady but very limited income. Living in poverty is a struggle in itself, and the struggle can be intensified when combined with some of the other problems caused by parenting with a mental illness.

There are times when someone with a mental illness has a diminished capacity to care for herself, let alone other people. While under the care of someone with a mental illness, the children in the home may be at risk for being neglected. They may not have regular access to meals and may live in an environment that is unclean or unsafe. They may not have access to regular health or dental care. Aside from these environmental and physical factors, there are interpersonal risk factors as well. Research suggests that some parents with mental illnesses have poor communication skills and may be likely to act aggressively at times.

Living with a parent or guardian with a mental illness can feel shameful to youth for several reasons. They may feel different from their peers with "normal" parents because their caregiver has odd behaviors or stays in bed all day. They may be aware that their home is messier and more disorganized than others they know. Children and teens tend to be self-focused, which results in feeling that everything is their fault. The brains of young people are often not capable of the kind of thought processes that help them reason. Rather than understanding

that the mental illness is just that—an illness—teens may think that if they were "better," their parents or guardians would feel better. Even as children mature into adolescence and eventually adulthood, they often carry these feelings of inadequacy and shame for years. And when children of caregivers who have a mental illness reach adulthood, they may experience problems maintaining healthy adult relationships, and have emotional difficulties that include feeling shame and guilt about their childhood, a pessimistic view about life, and poor self-esteem.

WHAT YOU CAN DO TO HELP

Understand Mental Illness

People whose parents have a mental illness may feel shame associated with society's misperceptions about people with mental illnesses, and feel they cannot tell others what happens at home. People with mental illnesses are portrayed in a poor light in the media. They are often unfairly stereotyped as deranged and violent.

There is a misconception that people with a mental illness act "crazy." This is not always the case. Many people with mental illness take medication, attend counseling, and keep their symptoms in check. Identifying a parent or guardian with a mental illness is not easy. Even if you do not meet the parent, listen to what the teen says about his caregiver for clues about what is going on at home. In many communities, you may come to know about a caregiver with a mental illness through gossip. Once you become aware that a teen is living with a person with a mental illness, it is important to build a relationship with the teen and offer your support. Knowing that a person has a mental illness can help you to be more sympathetic to the situation. Because you are working with teens, and not their parents and guardians, the goal should not be to "cure" the parent or guardian but rather to support and educate the teen.

Meet Basic Needs

Do what you can to ensure that the teen's basic needs are being met. Does she have food to eat? Does she have somewhere safe to live? Is she being physically harmed? Does she have appropriate clothing? Are her basic hygiene needs being met? If you are concerned that her essential needs are not being met, contact a local social services agency.

Connect

Make a connection with a teen in this situation. Ask him how he is doing and if he wants to talk about the situation at home. It is unlikely he will answer many questions about the parent or guardian, so keep your questions and comments focused on the teen. Be persistent with your offers to talk, but also respect his wish for privacy. Let the teen know that you are available for him when he is ready to talk. The more healthy adults the teen has in his life, the better off he will be. In addition, encourage the teen to notify an adult if the situation at home escalates. Make sure he knows about community crisis lines, appropriate times to call 911, and after-hours programs so he has resources if you are not available.

Educate Teens about Mental Illness

Often misconceptions about mental illness lead to shame and guilt. Help teens find out more information about the illness that their parent or guardian has been diagnosed with. Understanding what the symptoms look like can help a teen learn that it is a disease and not something she did to make her caregiver act in certain ways. Education about mental illnesses can also help her understand what her parent or guardian is going through and perhaps help predict what may seem like very unpredictable behaviors.

Get Professional Counseling

There are many feelings to deal with when you grow up with someone who has a mental illness. Encourage teens to see a professional counselor to work through some of these feelings. There may be a support group with other teens in this situation that can provide support and education.

Assure Teens That They Are Not to Blame

Teens are known for thinking the world revolves around them. Sadly, it is exactly this attitude that can cause teens to blame themselves for the illness. Reminding them as often as you can that their parents or guardians have an illness and that it isn't their fault will help them feel less guilty and ashamed.

Communicate with and Support Parents or Guardians

Building a relationship with the parent or guardian can help build a support system for the teen. You can also help the immediate family create a support system with their extended family members. It is helpful for teens to feel supported and loved by their parents; the more you support the parent so she can support the youth, the better the entire family system will be.

Provide Social Opportunities

Teens who grew up in a home with someone who has a mental illness may benefit from social skills education and opportunities to socialize with peers and positive adults. It is a good idea to model good personal boundaries and healthy emotional expression.

Help Them Help Themselves

Support teens in making new positive relationships and strengthening current positive relationships. Encourage relationships, activities, and interest in school. Reinforcing self-enriching activities will encourage the teen to continue on a positive path. These kids are at risk for developing a mental illness, so doing what you can to strengthen their coping skills and support systems is the best help you can give them.

RESOURCES

American Academy of Child and Adolescent Psychiatry: Facts for Children of Parents with Mental Illness (aacap.org).

Mental Health America (mentalhealthamerica.net). An organization dedicated to helping people live mentally healthier lives.

Emotional Illness in Your Family: Helping Your Relative, Helping Yourself by Harvey Roy Greenberg. New York: Macmillan, 1989.

Nothing to Be Ashamed of: Growing Up with Mental Illness in Your Family by Sherry H. Dinner. New York: Lothrop, Lee & Shepard Books, 1989.

Schizophrenia: Straight Talk for Family and Friends by Maryellen Walsh. New York: Morrow, 1985.

Toxic Parents: Overcoming Their Hurtful Legacy and Reclaiming Your Life by Susan Forward, with Craig Buck. New York: Bantam Books, 1989.

NOTES

1. Center for Mental Health Services Research, Substance Abuse and Mental Health Services Administration, "Critical Issues for Parents with Mental Illness and Their Families," (2001), mentalhealth.samhsa.gov/publications/allpubs/KEN-01-0109/default.asp (accessed September 19, 2007).

2. C. T. Mowbray and O. P. Mowbray, "Psychosocial Outcomes of Adult Children of Mothers with Depression and Bipolar Disorder," *Journal of Emotional and Behavioral Disorders*, 14 (2006): 130–142.

3. Mental Health America, "When a Parent Has a Mental Illness: From Risk to Resiliency—Protective Factors for Children," www.nmha.org/index.cfm?objectid= E3397A71-1372-4D20-C807F1A0E93C2812 (accessed September 19, 2007).

When Teens Have a Mentally Ill Parent or Caregiver

Learn the ways that symptoms of mental illness manifest in adults, and be aware that many illnesses can be managed with medication and counseling. Listen to what the teen says about his parent or guardian to understand what's going on at home. Build a relationship with the teen and provide support. Remember, the goal is to support the teen, not cure the caregiver.

Do what you can to ensure that the teen's basic needs are being met. Does she have food to eat? Does she have somewhere safe to live? If you suspect that her basic needs are not being met, contact a local social services agency.

Make a connection with the teen. Ask him how he is doing and if he wants to talk about the situation at home. Keep your questions focused on him, rather than on his parent or guardian. Let him know that you are available. Be persistent with your offers to talk, but also respect his wish for privacy.

Encourage him to notify an adult if the situation at home becomes more than he can deal with, and make sure he knows about community crisis lines, when to call 911, and after-hours care programs.

Help the teen find out more information about the illness that her parent or guardian has been diagnosed with. Understanding what the symptoms mean can help a teen better deal with the situation.

Encourage him to see a professional counselor to work through some of his feelings about living in a household with a mentally ill person. There may also be support groups available, which can reassure the teen that he is not the only one in this situation.

Remind the teen as often as you can that her parent or guardian has an illness and that it isn't her fault, or her parent or guardian's fault.

Support teens in making new positive relationships and strengthening current positive relationships. Reaching out to extended family or caring adults can strengthen his support network and help him feel more secure and loved.

PHYSICAL ABUSE

Child abuse and neglect are perpetrated upon children of all ages and in families from all backgrounds. In 2005, an estimated 3.3 million referrals, involving the alleged maltreatment of approximately 6 million children, were made to Child Protective Services (CPS) agencies. Of the cases where there was a determination of child abuse or neglect (899,000 children), more than half of the victims were 7 years old or younger; more than 15 percent of the victims suffered physical abuse; an estimated 1,460 children died due to child abuse or neglect; more than three-quarters of perpetrators of child maltreatment were parents; women composed a larger percentage of all perpetrators than men; and more than three-fourths of all perpetrators were younger than age 40.[1]

Although child abuse and neglect include physical, sexual, and emotional abuse, the purpose of this chapter is to focus on information and ideas for working with youth who are or have been physically abused. Physical abuse is characterized by physical injury, such as bruises and fractures that result from various forms of abuse. Physical abuse includes punching, beating, kicking, biting, shaking, throwing, stabbing, choking, hitting, and burning. The injury or injuries may have resulted from severe discipline or physical punishment that is inappropriate to the youth's age or condition; the injury may be the result of a single episode or repeated episodes that range in severity.[2]

Signs of Physical Abuse

You should consider the possibility of physical abuse when the youth and/or parent or caregiver exhibits signs of child abuse. These lists are not exhaustive, but we should consider the possibility of physical abuse when a youth

- Has unexplained burns, bites, bruises, broken bones, or black eyes.
- Has fading bruises or other marks noticeable after an absence from school.
- Seems frightened of the parent and protests when it's time to go home.
- Shrinks at the approach of adults.
- Shows sudden changes in behavior or school performance.
- Has not received help for physical or medical problems that were brought to the parent or guardian's attention.
- Has learning problems that cannot be attributed to specific physical or psychological causes.
- Is always watchful, as though preparing for something bad to happen.
- Lacks adult supervision.
- Is overcompliant, an overachiever, or takes responsibility beyond his years.

You should consider the possibility of physical abuse when the parent or other adult caregiver

- Offers conflicting or unconvincing explanations, or no explanation, for the youth's injury.
- Describes the youth as "evil" or in other very negative terms, or sees the youth as bad, worthless, or burdensome.

- Shows little concern for the youth, rarely responding to the school's requests for information, for conferences, or for home visits.

- Denies the existence of—or blames the youth for—the youth's problems in school or at home.

- Uses harsh physical discipline.

- Asks the teacher to use harsh physical discipline if the youth misbehaves.

- Demands perfection or a level of physical or academic performance the youth cannot achieve.

- Looks primarily to the youth for care, attention, and satisfaction of emotional needs.

- Has a history of being abused as a child.

If you suspect a teen has been abused because of any of these signs, or for other reasons that indicate abuse, contact CPS as soon as possible.

WHAT YOU CAN DO TO HELP

Know When and How to Report to Child Protective Services

Your obligations and agency protocols as either a mandated reporter or an employee of a program supersede any suggestions we will provide. You may live in a state where all citizens are mandated reporters, or work under a professional license or agency that requires you to report any and all suspicions of child abuse or neglect, or may simply be someone who isn't sure what to do with your concerns about a youth who is possibly being abused or neglected. Anyone who suspects child abuse or neglect can and should report those suspicions to the local CPS agency. You do not need to be positive that abuse has happened—rather, your suspicion a youth has been abused is grounds to file a CPS report. Reporting suspected abuse or neglect isn't accusing a parent of being a bad parent, it's taking action on your concern for a youth. It is the role of CPS to assess if abuse has occurred.

Reporting suspicions of abuse or neglect to your CPS agency does not make you responsible for investigating a case, and you shouldn't attempt to gather evidence unless that role is specified by your profession. Your role as a reporter is to provide unbiased, factual information about why you suspect abuse or neglect. You can provide social services with the youth's name, age, address, and other basic demographic information without breaching confidentiality.

Reluctance to Report

Challenge yourself on your rationale for *not* reporting child abuse. Some people don't report abuse due to fear of reprisal from the alleged perpetrator, fear that the youth will be removed unwillingly from the home, distrust of the system(s) that will process the teen's case, or anxieties about the outcome of the investigation. Please don't let these reservations stop you from reporting. If for any reason you are unsure whether or not you should report, contact your local CPS agency, share your suspicions, and ask them whether or not your concern is reportable. You will likely need to file both a verbal report over the phone and a written report with CPS. Contact your local CPS agency for copies of the forms to fill out when preparing child abuse reports. Keep extras on hand for all staff to access. If you file a CPS report, you should inform your supervisor of your action or do whatever your protocol requires.

"How adults responded to me sharing about the physical and sexual abuse that happened affected what and how much I would say. Adults who maintained patience and weren't afraid to ask me questions helped me build trust in others." —Heidi

Maintain Your Composure During Disclosures

Your reaction to a youth disclosing any form of abuse is instrumental to his well-being. In the moment of having a teen show you or share with you what has happened to him, you may want to throw up, scream, cry, and/or make promises you can't keep ("no one will ever do this to you again"). Acknowledge these thoughts and feelings to yourself and set them aside. Remind yourself that the teen is showing great trust and courage in disclosing the abuse, and your focus should be on what the teen is thinking and feeling. Ensure that you have opportunities to process disclosures of abuse with your supervisor or administrator rather than processing your experience with the teen. You can send a message of hope by maintaining your composure; you never want to send a message to a teen that what has happened to him is too overwhelming or too damaging for him to survive.

Understand Why Youth Don't Tell

Teens may choose not to voice that they were or are being abused for many reasons. Disclosures of abuse and the involvement of child welfare agencies often result in many changes to a family. Most youth, in spite of the abuse, do not want to divide their families, and often feel responsible for any changes and disruptions that occur, and they therefore remain silent about the abuse. Teens may still feel loyal to the abusive parent, or choose not to tell due to a fear of increased abuse and punishment. Teens may fear that no one will believe they are being abused, or believe they can protect their siblings from the abuse by being the abuser's primary target. Teens can feel responsible for the abuse, and in this belief take responsibility for lessening abuse toward others in the home.

Understand Cultural Differences in Parenting Styles vs. Child Abuse

Parenting behaviors are culturally defined, and cultural differences can lead to serious disagreements about what is appropriate or necessary with regard to parenting techniques. Actions thought to be normal or appropriate in one culture may be interpreted as abuse or neglect by another culture.[3] Cultural differences in parenting and definitions of abuse and neglect are complex issues that go beyond the scope of this brief overview, but one example of cultural practices being viewed as child abuse is *cao gio* ("coining"), a traditional form of healing used in the Southeast Asian community as a treatment for cold-type symptoms. After heated ointments are rubbed into the chest, back, or head, "A coin or the back of a spoon is then rubbed vigorously in a linear fashion for 15 to 20 minutes over the spine, along the ribs, or until a reddened area appears. This practice is felt to release a 'bad wind.'" Scrapes or bruises, or sometimes even minor burns, may result. *Cao gio* has been misidentified as child abuse in several cases.[4]

> "I didn't tell people about the abuse for a long time because I was afraid of the unknown, I was afraid of what would happen to my life. I didn't know what would happen to me or my dad, I needed to know I was not in trouble." —Alyssa

Invest time learning more about the parenting norms of each group you work with so you can better understand the many cultural differences in parenting. A resource to expand your knowledge in this area is the book *Child Abuse and Culture: Working with Diverse Families* by Lisa Aronson Fontes (New York: Guilford Press, 2005).

While child abuse happens in families from all backgrounds, your concerns about child abuse may be due to cultural differences in discipline, and may not be considered child abuse by CPS. Some states and provinces have exceptions to their definitions of abuse and neglect that include cultural practices and cultural values. Check with your local CPS agency to learn if your state or province includes these exceptions. If you are faced with a specific concern and are unsure whether something would be considered abuse or considered a cultural difference in parenting, contact CPS and share your concerns: they will determine whether or not you need to report your suspicion of abuse or neglect. Refrain from misjudging parenting behaviors by learning as much as you can about definitions of child abuse and the cultural context a parenting practice may stem from. Work with families to provide information and assistance to help them understand the definitions of child abuse and neglect in the United States and Canada. In addition to readings on cultural differences in parenting, invite families to share their cultural norms with you. Do not be afraid to educate them about the definitions, laws, and cultural practices of the place they currently reside. It may also be helpful to provide contact information for multicultural counselors who are available to work with clients whose primary language is not English.

"I had friends and coaches who would ask about my bruises, but I always had an excuse. I carried a lot of guilt because I didn't tell the truth. Adults need to know that just because they expressed their concern it doesn't end there. They need to keep their eye on their concern and not take what teens say at face value." —Joelle

RESOURCES

American Professional Society on the Abuse of Children (APSAC) (apsac.org).

Child Welfare League of America (cwla.org).
Phone: 202-638-2952.

Childhelp USA (childhelpusa.org). Phone: 480-922-8212.

Covenant House Nineline. Phone: 800-999-9999.
A 24-hour hotline to talk about concerns such as abuse, suicide, and running away.

National Child Abuse Hotline. Phone: 800-25-ABUSE.

National Youth Violence Prevention (safeyouth.org).
Web site contains great handouts for parents, educators, and more.

Parents Anonymous (parentsanonymous.org). Phone: 909-621-6184 ext. 222. Call for info on Parents Anonymous groups in your area. A child abuse prevention organization dedicated to strengthening families and building caring communities that support safe and nurturing homes for all children.

Prevent Child Abuse America (preventchildabuse.org).
Phone: 312-663-3520.

Child Abuse and Culture: Working with Diverse Families,
by Lisa Aronson Fontes. New York: Guilford Press, 2005.

Splintered Emotions: Aftermath of Child Abuse,
by Trena Cole. Indianapolis: Oberpark Publishing, 2006.

NOTES

1. U.S. Department of Health and Human Services, Administration on Children, Youth and Families, *Child Maltreatment 2005* (Washington, DC: U.S. Government Printing Office, 2007), 16–17.

2. Child Welfare Information Gateway, "Physical Abuse." Adapted from J. Goldman, M. K. Salus, D. Wolcott, and K. Y. Kennedy, *A Coordinated Response to Child Abuse and Neglect: The Foundation for Practice* (Washington, DC: U.S. Department of Health and Human Services, 2003), www.childwelfare.gov/pubs/usermanuals/foundation/foundationc.cfm (accessed October 21, 2007).

3. Bridging Refugee Youth and Children's Services, April 2005 Spotlight, "Determining Child Abuse and Neglect across Cultures," www.brycs.org/brycs_spotapr2005.htm (accessed October 22, 2007).

4. Stanford School of Medicine, "Frequently Asked Questions for the Stanford Medical Center Community," childabuse.stanford.edu/faq.html (accessed January 22, 2008).

When and How to Report to Child Protective Services

Anyone who suspects child abuse or neglect can and should report their suspicions to their local Child Protective Services (CPS) agency. You do not need to be positive abuse has happened—rather, your suspicion a youth has been abused is grounds to file a CPS report.

Reporting suspicions of abuse or neglect to your CPS agency does not make you responsible for investigating a case, and you shouldn't attempt to gather evidence unless that role is specified by your profession. Your role as a reporter is to provide the governing agency with unbiased, factual information about why you suspect abuse or neglect.

If you are unsure whether or not you should report abuse, for whatever reason, contact your local CPS agency and share your concerns with them. Ask them whether or not you have a reportable concern.

You will likely need to file both a verbal report over the phone and a written report with CPS. Contact your local CPS agency for copies of the forms to fill out when doing child abuse reports. Have the forms on hand for all staff to access. If you file a CPS report, you should inform your supervisor.

The Abuse of Children Wheel

The Abuse of Children Wheel was developed by the Domestic Abuse Intervention Project of Duluth, Minnesota. Each segment of the wheel describes a way in which an abuser can exert power over his or her victim, while the outer edge of the wheel contains a list of abusive behaviors. The wheel is designed to serve as a visual reference and reminder of the ways abuse can manifest and the reasons why it persists.

Domestic Abuse Intervention Project • 202 East Superior Street • Duluth, Minnesota 55802 • 218-722-2781 • www.duluth-model.org

PREGNANCY

Teen pregnancy is a divisive issue that many people struggle with. You and the teens you work with may have very different perspectives when it comes to pregnancy, abortion, and adoption options, and this chapter is intended to provide information about all three choices in as unbiased a manner as possible. If you find you are uncomfortable when it comes to working with teens who are dealing with these issues, remember that it is always acceptable and appropriate to refer them to another person or organization that specializes in these topics.

The United States has the highest rates of teen pregnancy and births in the western industrialized world. The adolescent pregnancy rate in the United States is nearly twice that of Canada and Great Britain and approximately four times that of France and Sweden.[1] Teen pregnancy, birth, and abortion rates in the United States have been declining since 1991; recent surveys indicate a slight increase in the rate of teen pregnancy, but it is too soon to tell if this is a trend. In 1982, there were 107 births for every 1,000 teenagers aged 15 to 19; the rate dropped to 40.5 births per 1,000 teenagers in 2005;[2] in 2006, the rate increased slightly to 41.9 births per 1,000 teenagers.[3] The decline in teen pregnancy in the last decade is due to more consistent contraceptive use and higher proportions of teens choosing to delay sexual activity.[4]

WHAT YOU CAN DO TO HELP

This discussion assumes you are not a pregnancy options counselor. Even if you've had no training in this area, there's a good chance that you have worked or will work with teens who share that they are not sure what to do about their pregnancies. These suggestions are intended to make your conversations more useful to the teen who is pregnant.

This discussion also focuses primarily on working with girls and young women who are faced with an unintended pregnancy, but that does not mean that boys and young men are irrelevant in these situations. They may also need support and caring from an adult, and have feelings to process about the situation. When reading this chapter, keep in mind that a pregnant teen may want to actively include her partner in her decision-making process, and that he may be just as uncertain and overwhelmed as she is.

Be Aware of Your Morals, Political Views, and Opinions

Most of us have strong feelings and beliefs about pregnancy options. If a teen shares that she doesn't know what to do, be mindful of your beliefs, and remember—this is her pregnancy. Your beliefs are incredibly important—they are equally as important as hers—but again, this is *her* pregnancy. We cannot assume that what we believe would be best for us is what would be best for others. It's more likely a teen will state, "I don't know what to do" rather than, "Tell me what to do." Hear what the teen is saying. Many ethical codes in human services require the provider to withhold her personal beliefs to better serve people as individuals. Adherence to this principle removes the dynamic of "knowing best" and allows the conversation to be focused on the teen.

Conversing with a teen about pregnancy options should be free of a predetermined decision that you believe is best. While we may keep our beliefs silent, we may be tempted to overtly or covertly guide the conversation to the decision we believe is best. What a pregnant teen needs most in these conversations is understanding and support. If you feel yourself guiding a youth to one choice, heighten your awareness of her language, her emotions, and her needs. Supporting youth on their journey is more beneficial than determining their journey.

Make Appropriate Referrals

Compile a list of local and national resources on the three pregnancy options: abortion, adoption, and parenting to share with teens. Be well informed about and fair to all three choices in your referrals, and be aware that many pregnancy options counseling agencies have a biased orientation to which choice is best. By providing teens with a comprehensive list of resources, they can direct their questions to specific agencies, rather than to you.

Leave Your Assumptions at Home

All too often adults scorn and look down on pregnant teens and minor parents with a "What was she thinking?" message. Eighty-two percent of teen pregnancies are unplanned; they account for about one in five of all unintended pregnancies annually.[5] Refrain from reducing teen pregnancy to "What was she thinking?" as it blinds you to exploring what may really be going on in a teen's life. Although many teens engage in consensual sex, the pregnancy may be the result of rape, incest, prostitution, or sexual promiscuity related to being sexually abused. The aforementioned issues are often laden with guilt and shame, so don't anticipate that the teen will disclose the "real" reason she's pregnant.

Abortion

Deciding whether or not to have an abortion can be an emotional and difficult thing. Knowing your state laws on consent and waiting periods, being aware of transportation and financial issues, understanding the emotional ramifications, and shar-ing all that information with the teen can help her make a more informed decision.

If a teen chooses to have an abortion, she'll likely deal with a variety of issues and potential barriers to this choice. In the United States, access to abortion services varies by state (in Canada, there are no legal restrictions to obtaining an abortion). Individual state law will define whether patients seeking an abortion must go through a 24-hour (or longer) waiting period between talking to a doctor and proceeding with the abortion. When minors seek an abortion, some states require notification of one or both parents, and/or consent from one or both parents. (In certain instances teens may be able to obtain a judicial bypass, which allows a minor to receive approval from the courts to have an abortion rather than getting parental consent.) Many states also have restrictions on how late in a pregnancy an abortion can be performed, and since a teen may not realize she is pregnant until several weeks after the pregnancy begins, limited time to follow these legal procedures can be a difficulty as well.

Abortion clinics can be hard to reach. In some states there are only one or two abortion providers, usually located in large cities, and it may require a day's travel to reach them. She may need someone to accompany her to the appointment and help her understand after-care instructions, or she may need someone to act as an interpreter. Finally, abortions are not necessarily covered by health insurance, or a teen may not wish to charge an abortion to her insurance for fear of discovery.

A teen considering or choosing abortion will likely struggle with emotional concerns as well. Her religious upbringing may forbid or discourage abortion, her family or partner may oppose it, or she may be personally struggling with wanting to have an abortion, even though she had previously considered herself against it. A teen may also be fearful of facing protesters outside a clinic, or worried that people will find out she had an abortion. After the procedure, she may deal with unexpected feelings of relief, guilt, sadness, anger, and shame, and she may need assistance in dealing with these emotions.

Adoption

A teen who is considering or choosing adoption also faces a variety of issues specific to this choice. She will face major decisions, such as which adoption agency to work with, whether she wants an open or closed adoption, and, if she chooses open adoption, how much contact she wants with the adoptive family. Teens will also have to tell their families if they are choosing adoption, which may be a conversation they will need your assistance in preparing for.

A teen who chooses adoption will also have to simultaneously prepare for delivery and for giving up the child shortly after delivery. She may need someone to share her worries, exhaustion, and sadness with. A teen who chooses adoption will also likely face other people's assumptions that she is keeping the child ("Are you excited? Why aren't you in the minor parents group?") and if she shares her choice, may also face questioning from adults and peers about why she is choosing adoption. Once the adoption has been completed, a teen may experience a wide range of emotions, from relief to guilt to anger. Just as with someone who has had an abortion, a teen who decides to place her child for adoption may need assistance in coping with these feelings.

Teen Parenting

Being a minor parent catapults adolescents into adult responsibilities, but they are still adolescents. Statements and beliefs such as, "Well, if he was old enough to get a girl pregnant, he's old enough to figure this out," should be confronted with an awareness that pregnancy and parenthood do not result in a teen's magically skipping through developmental stages. Minor parents need the same healthy and supportive guidance and structure all other teens need. Encourage adherence to the same rules and structures that existed before they became parents. Acknowledge the responsibilities they are taking on and the difficulty and courage in changing priorities. Allow teens to grieve over what they have to give up in order to be parents. Recognize that like their peers, teen parents may be preoccupied with their social lives, their appearance, and their own material needs. Acknowledge the social changes that occur with becoming a parent, and assist teens with finding a healthy balance between their own developmental impulses and the necessary sacrifices of parenting.

Assist with Coordinating Medical Care

Babies born to teens are more likely to have medical and developmental concerns. Some teens go without or receive very late prenatal care, due to reasons such as trying to hide a pregnancy, being without insurance, moving frequently, or discovering a pregnancy late. Be committed to ensuring that teens receive prenatal care. Check with your county to see if it provides medical assistance to pregnant teens. Contact your school nurse to see if he or she is aware of medical options for teens without insurance. If all else fails, call your local hospital and, with consent, let them know you are working with a teen who needs immediate care at minimal cost. While it is important to focus on the needs of the teen, prenatal care is nonnegotiable. If you know a teen has been without prenatal care, help her make a doctor's appointment immediately. If necessary, assist with arranging transportation. Do all you can to eliminate her barriers to health care.

Encourage Lifestyle Changes

For many women and girls, being pregnant means halting not-so-healthy lifestyle choices. Provide encouragement and support for these changes. Smoking, drinking, drug use, excessive caffeine consumption, minimal sleep, unsafe sex, unhealthy diet, lack of exercise, and stress can be harmful to a fetus (and the mother). While eliminating these things from our lives can be difficult for adults, doing so can much harder for adolescents. Acknowledge the difficulty in these changes and help teens stick with the adjustments they make. Encourage these changes post-pregnancy as well, as most of those unhealthy choices could compromise parenting skills or be unhealthy in a child-care environment.

Help Plan for the Future

Planning for the future should include all domains of a teen's life: medical, educational, financial, social, sexual, and familial. Encourage pregnant teens to talk to their health-care providers about subsequent birth control *before* the baby is born. Talk about the necessity for ongoing medical care for infants and the importance of scheduling these appointments in advance. Support the teen in finishing high school and inquire whether her school provides tutoring during maternity leave. Initiate ongoing conversations about educational and career goals beyond high school, and coordinate teens with guidance counselors. Minor parents should not be solely defined by parenthood: continuously provide hope and support the idea that they have a future. While teen parents, especially boys, may think the responsible thing to do (and it might be) is to "just get a job" to support the baby, help them understand that they have a wide variety of options to reach further educational and career goals, such as working for a year to save money before college, attending classes part-time, or enrolling in special programs or housing for young parents. Help teen parents plot out not only the long-term obstacles they may face but also the long-term benefits of making optimistic decisions for the future, such as a higher salary, better living conditions, and increased job opportunities.

Explore and Expand Their Support System

The traditional systems of support are not always available to teenage parents. A teen girl may no longer be in a relationship with the child's biological father, and an infant may place tremendous stress on the teenager's relationships with her own parents. A teen boy may find that previously supportive adults now resist supporting him as a parent, leaving the teen to feel increased isolation and abandonment. Encourage teen parents to connect with many resources, including extended family members, pediatricians, mentors, early childhood family education classes, and teachers.

Provide Parenting Information

Encourage teen parents to educate themselves about healthy parenting and their child's developmental needs. Provide them with information on local parenting classes or support groups and assist with coordinating transportation barriers. If possible, have parenting resources on-site, such as parenting books teens can check out of a resource library and parenting or family magazines. Make copies of parenting articles for all parents you work with.

RESOURCES

The Abortion Clinic Directory (ru486.com). Assists with finding an abortion provider throughout the United States.

Being a Teenage Parent (baby-place.com/teen_parents. php). Links to teen parent sites and information.

Child Welfare Information Gateway (childwelfare.gov). 800-394-3366. Formerly the National Adoption Information Clearinghouse. Provides access to information and resources. Includes national foster care and adoption directory.

Mom, Dad, I'm Pregnant . . . (momdadimpregnant.com). Information to help teens talk to their parents about pregnancy, and information for parents with pregnant teens.

Women, Infants, and Children (WIC) (fns.usda.gov/wic). Site includes toll-free numbers, addresses, and e-mail addresses for all WIC state agencies.

Pregnancy Options Workbook: A Resource for Women Making a Difficult Decision (pregnancyoptions.info). This workbook, which you can download from the Web site, provides an accurate, nonbiased platform for teens to explore what they are feeling, their support network, religious/spiritual concerns, and making a pregnancy decision. All pregnancy options are explored.

NOTES

1. S. Singh and J. E. Darroch, "Adolescent Pregnancy and Childbearing: Levels and Trends in Developed Countries," *Family Planning Perspectives* 32 (1999): 14–23.

2. Guttmacher Institute, *U.S. Teenage Pregnancy Statistics: National and State Trends and Trends by Race and Ethnicity*, 2006, www.guttmacher.org/pubs/2006/09/12/USTPstats .pdf (accessed October 8, 2007).

3. B. E. Hamilton, J. A. Martin, and S. J. Ventura, "Births: Preliminary Data for 2006," *National Vital Statistics Reports* 56, no. 7 (2007).

4. J. S. Santelli, L. Duberstein-Lindberg, L. B. Finer, and S. Singh, "Explaining Recent Declines in Adolescent Pregnancy in the United States: The Contribution of Abstinence and Improved Contraceptive Use," *American Journal of Public Health* 97 (2007): 1–7.

5. L. B. Finer and S. K. Henshaw, "Disparities in Rates of Unintended Pregnancy in the United States, 1994 and 2001," *Perspectives on Sexual and Reproductive Health* 38 (2006): 90–96.

Strategies for Working with Teens
Who Are Exploring Pregnancy Options

Be aware of your morals, political views, and opinions. If a teen shares that she doesn't know what to do, be mindful of your beliefs and remember, this is *her* pregnancy.

Make appropriate referrals. Compile a list of local and national resources on the three pregnancy options: abortion, adoption, and parenting. Be fair to all three choices in your referrals.

Remember, pregnant teens are still teens. Even though they face some very adult concerns and decisions, pregnant teenagers have the same developmental needs as their peers. Be patient as they work through priorities.

If teens choose to become parents, provide information on local parenting classes or support groups and assist with eliminating transportation barriers.

SELF-INJURY

Self-injury (also called self-harm or self-mutilation) is the act of deliberately causing harm or damage to one's body in an attempt to alter one's mood or state of mind. Self-injury is usually not suicidal behavior, but it is a serious issue. Often the injuring behaviors include cutting, carving, burning, hair pulling, picking at skin or reopening scabs, bruising, breaking bones (especially fingers or toes), or hitting oneself with objects. When people hurt themselves for sexual gratification or body decorating (as in the case of tattooing or body piercing), it is not considered self-injury.

Most people who self-injure do so in private and try to keep it a secret. Self-injury may range from mild to severe. There may be superficial cuts, or sometimes injuries may be so severe the person requires medical attention. Many people who self-injure will go to great lengths to hide their scars, bruises, and burn marks. People will often cut, burn, and otherwise injure parts of their body that are easily concealed by clothing. It is not always obvious that someone is engaging in self-injurious behaviors.

Who Self-Injures?

It is estimated that as many as 4 percent of the population of the United States has engaged in occasional self-mutilating behavior, and as many as 21 percent of people from a clinical sample have engaged in self-mutilating behaviors.[1] People who self-injure come from all walks of life. People of every race, gender, socioeconomic status, sexual orientation, age, education level, and religion self-injure—but self-injury is most often seen in ado-

lescent females and women in their twenties with average or above-average intelligence. Other common factors of people who self-injure may include a history of abuse, growing up in a family that suppresses anger or other emotions, substance use, and a lack of a social support system. Self-injury has also been linked to the mental illness diagnoses of borderline personality disorder, obsessive-compulsive disorder, eating disorders, and depression. Again, it is important to note that anyone may be someone who self-injures.

> "I never cut to kill myself, I cut because I felt numb inside, constantly. I cut to feel alive, to know I was an actual person. It made the pain of the sexual abuse go away, just for a little bit."
> —Taylor

There are some indicators that may alert you that someone is self-injuring. If a young person is wearing long pants and long-sleeved shirts when the weather is warm, she may be trying to hide fresh injuries or scars. You may find razors, lighters, or sharp objects that seem out of place. Frequent, unexplained injuries may actually be self-inflicted (be cautious—this is also a sign that she may be a victim of violence by others). Another sign may be the young person's wanting excessive time alone behind closed doors. Finally, if someone finds dried blood on the inside of her clothes or in her bedroom, you might suspect self-injury. Listen to your gut: if you suspect something is wrong or different, it just might be.

Why Do People Self-Injure?

There are many reasons people self-injure, but typically it is a means of altering a person's mood state. Self-injury can be viewed as an ineffective coping skill. If a person is overwhelmed by emotion, self-injury may help them gain relief from these intense feelings. Many people who self-injure report that they experience an immediate relief from their emotional pain after inflicting physical pain.

Sometimes people self-injure because they feel emotionally numb. Self-injury is a way to feel something, and allows the person who self-injures to feel alive or feel like a real person. People might also self-injure because they feel they deserve to be hurt or punished. They may feel they need to punish themselves for bad feelings and emotions, or they may just want to punish themselves because they hate themselves.

Another reason people might self-injure is to externalize their emotional pain. They injure themselves on the outside as a way of showing that they are hurting on the inside, or to feel pain on the outside instead of on the inside.

Self-injury may be used as a way of managing and controlling emotional pain. When a person has emotional pain, he often feels that he has little control over how that pain began or when that pain appears. When one intentionally inflicts pain on himself, he is in control of those sensations. There may be any number of reasons a person hurts himself, but it is important to keep in mind that he may not be consciously aware of those reasons. Discovering the reasons behind the self-injury will be important during the recovery process.

How Do Self-Injury Behaviors Develop?

People may wonder how a young person begins to use self-injury as a coping mechanism. Often, youth who self-injure try it for the first time after hearing about others who self-injure. Sometimes the first self-injury occurrence happens by accident. Some young people try self-injury a couple of times and find it doesn't "work" for them. For other youth, self-injury can become addictive.

Self-injurious behavior can become a cycle that is difficult to stop. Strong emotions such as anger, shame, fear, guilt, or anxiety build up, and the person seeks a way to make them stop. Instead of dealing with these emotions in a more constructive manner, self-injury is used as a coping mechanism. Once people injure themselves, they experience immediate relief, but soon after the event they begin to feel ashamed about what they have done. They try to conceal the behaviors and the scars, and the emotions begin to build again. Despite the fact that self-injuring behaviors cause shame, they become a way for people to feel relief from their pain. The cycle continues and the self-injury behaviors may increase in intensity and frequency.

Misconceptions and Myths about Self-Injury

There are two common misconceptions about self-injury that need to be addressed: that self-injury is the same as a suicide attempt, and that self-injury is just attention-getting behavior. Both of these misconceptions can hinder efforts at recovery.

Self-injury and attempting suicide may look similar on the outside, but they are not synonymous. While both may result in an injury that may be life threatening, the reasons behind self-injurious behavior and a suicide attempt may be very different. Often, self-injuring is a coping mechanism that allows the person to soothe out-of-control emotions and avoid attempting to kill herself. According to Deb Martinson, author and chair of the American Self-Harm Information Clearinghouse, people who have self-injured have been more harmed than helped by professionals assuming they were suicidal. They may be forced into an unnecessary emergency hospitalization or extensive psychiatric care. It is important to know how severe the injuries inflicted are, because the young person who is hurting her- or himself may unintentionally inflict an injury so severe it may result in serious harm or death. But it is vital that people not overreact and treat self-injury in the same manner they would a suicide attempt. Listening and not reacting excessively will help guide you through this trying time.

While it is important not to overreact when faced with a young person who is self-injuring, it is just as important *not* to ignore self-injurious behavior or dismiss the act as a simple manipulation for attention. While self-injury may be an attempt to communicate hurt feelings on the inside, it is usually not an attempt to control others or "act out."

WHAT YOU CAN DO TO HELP

Listen

If you know a young person who is self-injuring, there are things you can do to help. Remember that self-injury is one way of maintaining control of frightening emotions and a method of soothing the self. Probably the most important thing you can do is listen to the young person who is self-injuring—don't be quick to judge! Talk to the young person about how he is feeling and inquire about the issues and problems he is experiencing now. It is critical to show that you care.

Don't advocate punishment for the person for hurting herself and don't attempt to force her to stop what she is doing. While the goal is to eventually stop the self-injuring behaviors, trying to exert control over the young person's behaviors will only contribute to her feelings of helplessness. It is also important not to "shame" the person who is self-injuring. Telling a young person that what she is doing is stupid will only make her feel worse. Most people who self-injure know that they are making a poor choice and feel ashamed already. It is appropriate to tell the young person you are sorry she is hurting and you want to help her make better choices. Trying to understand the behavior rather than control it will increase communication between you and the person engaging in self-injury.

Encourage the young person to express his emotions. Sometimes people are discouraged from sharing emotions—particularly negative emotions. Allowing a young person to vent his anger, cry, or otherwise let his feelings out will help relieve some of the pressure that builds before he feels that self-injury is the only option. While the young person is expressing his emotions, try to remain objective and supportive. Don't take his anger or sadness personally. It is essential for the person who is self-injuring to feel that he can release his emotions without being judged.

Offer Help

Let the young person know you are willing to help her try to stop hurting herself and offer to find her the professional help she needs. Professional help is required in this situation, and might include seeing a counselor, psychologist, or therapist. There may also be group counseling or a support group available. While in counseling, the young person may gain insight into why she hurts herself. She may also identify the "triggers" that lead her to self-injure. She may explore issues in her past, such as abuse, and learn new coping skills. Even when she is in contact with professional help such as a counselor or therapist, continue to be supportive to her.

Help the young person find alternatives to self-injury. Working with the young person to create a list of alternative behaviors may help him to avoid self-injury the next time he feels the urge to hurt himself. Some creative alternatives include:

- Exercising
- Speed-writing (writing down feelings unfiltered while listening to loud, fast music)
- Taking a cool shower
- Drawing
- Working with clay
- Coloring
- Dancing crazily to a favorite song
- Tearing up magazines or newspapers
- Calling friends

- Journaling
- Reading
- Participating in a hobby
- Hitting a pillow
- Screaming into a pillow
- E-mailing friends or other supportive people

It is best to have the young person create a list of alternatives to self-injury that he finds meaningful. It's best to create this list when he is not in a time of crisis.

However you choose to help, it is important always to maintain an attitude of support. There are help and hope for those who self-injure, and your support may be the first step in the end of the self-injury cycle.

RESOURCES

American Self-Harm Information Clearinghouse (selfinjury.org).

Comes the Darkness, Comes the Light: A Memoir of Cutting, Healing, and Hope by Vanessa Vega. New York: AMACOM, 2007.

Inside a Cutter's Mind: Understanding and Helping Those Who Self-Injure by Jerusha Clark and Earl R. Henslin. Colorado Springs, CO: Th1nk, 2007.

The Scarred Soul: Understanding and Ending Self-Inflicted Violence by Tracy Alderman. Oakland, CA: New Harbinger Publications: Distributed in the United States by Publishers Group West, 1997.

Scars That Wound, Scars That Heal: A Journey Out of Self-Injury by Jan Kern. Cincinnati, OH: Standard Publishing, 2007.

Stranger in My Skin by Alysa Phillips. Minneapolis: Word Warriors Press, 2006.

Women Living with Self-Injury by Jane Wegscheider Hyman. Philadelphia: Temple University Press, 1999.

NOTES

1. J. Briere and E. Gil, "Self-Mutilation in Clinical and General Population Samples: Prevalence, Correlates and Functions," *American Journal of Orthopsychiatry* 68 (1998): 609–620.

Helping Someone Who Self-Injures

Listen and Support

Talk to the young person who is injuring her- or himself. Some sample questions include:

- How long have you been hurting yourself?
- What leads to your hurting yourself?
- How do you hurt yourself?
- Who else knows that you hurt yourself?
- Who would you be comfortable talking to about this?
- How can I help you with this problem?

Don't Overreact or Punish

- Acting shocked or "grossed out" increases shame and embarrassment.
- Punishing and forbidding self-injury increases loss of control and often takes away the person's main coping skill.

Refer

- Self-injury is a serious issue that requires professional help. Help find someone who specializes in self-injury.
- If the young person's injuries are severe, get him or her medical attention.
- Make sure you notify other professionals in your organization as required.

Engage the Young Person

- Doing activities is a great support—spend time doing fun things together: go out for ice cream, go for a walk, or do anything else the young person enjoys doing.

Find Alternatives and Help Create an Emergency Kit

- Help the young person develop a list of alternatives to hurting her- or himself, especially when he or she is most vulnerable to these feelings.
- The young person can decide what will go in the emergency kit. You can help gather the materials and even decorate the kit. Things to include could be:
  - Markers
  - Crayons
  - Paper
  - Pictures of friends and families
  - Clippings from magazines of soothing pictures
  - A CD of favorite songs
  - Letters from you, from friends, and other supportive people
  - A list of phone numbers and e-mail addresses of friends and other supportive people

SEXUAL ABUSE

According to reliable studies on sexual abuse, as many as 1 in 3 girls and 1 in 7 boys will be sexually abused before age 18.[1] Sexual abuse is perpetrated upon children from all types of backgrounds by offenders from all types of backgrounds.

According to the American Psychological Association, there is no universal definition of sexual abuse. Sexual abuse may include fondling genitals, masturbation, oral-genital contact, digital penetration, and vaginal and anal intercourse. It is not solely restricted to physical contact and may include exposure, voyeurism, and child pornography.[2] It's important to remember that there are touching and nontouching forms of sexual abuse, and neither form of sexual abuse should be minimized. Perpetrators of sexual abuse, and all abuse, use power and control over the victim. While most sexual abuse is perpetrated by adults, it can also be perpetrated by other minors, such as in cases of date or acquaintance rape and sibling incest. The emotional trauma that results from the type(s) of abuse varies from youth to youth.

Because of the numbers of youth victimized by sexual abuse, it is almost certain that you will work with a teen who has been or who is being sexually abused. Many youth never disclose their sexual abuse. The suggestions in this chapter will hopefully heighten your "radar" for sexual abuse and aid you in helping a teen that you are concerned has experienced sexual abuse.

WHAT YOU CAN DO TO HELP

Become Aware of the Warning Signs for Sexual Abuse

Becoming aware of the warning signs for sexual abuse is a powerful tool for knowing when you may need to contact your local child protection or social service agency. The presence of one warning sign does not mean a teen is being sexually abused, but you should become concerned if warning signs appear over a period of time and/or multiple signs are present. (However, some youth who are being sexually abused exhibit none of these signs.) Indicators for sexual abuse include (adapted from *Indicators of Child Sexual Abuse*, by the Rape & Abuse Crisis Center of Fargo-Moorhead):

- Withdrawal from family, friends, and activities
- Anger/aggression toward family members, friends, or pets
- Running away
- Lack of trust
- Advanced or unusual sexual knowledge and/or behavior for youth's age
- Nightmares
- Sudden refusal to change clothes in the locker room or engage in physical activities
- Sudden change in appetite and/or weight

- Becomes pregnant or contracts an STD/STI at an early age

- Depression and/or anxiety

- Suicidal ideation or attempts

- Self-harm, such as cutting or burning

- Unusual fears (e.g., fear of certain locations)

- Low self-esteem

- Increase in somatic complaints, such as headaches[3]

Be Aware That Signs of Sexual Abuse Vary

The preceding list of warning signs for sexual abuse focuses on the less socially acceptable ways teens cope with sexual abuse, but we must not dismiss teens who employ more socially accepted coping skills, such as becoming an overachiever. Challenge any beliefs you may hold that a youth who has been sexually abused will clearly display signs of trauma. Be aware that teens who are sexually abused can take routes in life that do not cause obvious concern to others. Be mindful that just because a teen is doing the "right things" doesn't mean he isn't hurting. Sexual abuse can affect a person's core beliefs about himself and the world; some teens work to create a façade so no one knows how horrible they feel inside.

We must also be careful not to make assumptions that what we see is what is always happening. An adult who is compliant with your program and/or seemingly active in a youth's life is not necessarily a nonabuser. Abusive people often choose to present themselves as nonabusive to the outside world.

Become Aware of Natural and Healthy Sexual Behaviors

Just as vital as knowing the warning signs of sexual abuse is knowing what is "normal" sexual behavior for youth at different stages of development. Knowing what is natural and healthy prevents us from jumping to conclusions about sexual abuse, and provides us with a context for understanding the sexual behaviors that youth may exhibit. See the

resource portion of this chapter for recommended readings on youth's sexual behaviors.

Avoid Physical Contact

Many of us would feel awkward not reaching out to a youth—through hugs, pats on the back, touches on the shoulder, even horseplay. While these means of displaying care may be innocent and seem comforting, they can be frightening to a teen who has been abused. It is best to refrain from physical contact with youth unless the teen has given consent or the contact is initiated by the teen. Be creative in finding new ways to show a teen you care without touching.

> "I was the kid people wanted their kids to be like. Someone once asked me 'What did your parents do to get things so right?' I didn't want them to do anything my dad did. People believed he was a perfect parent."
> —Anne

Provide Lessons on Sexual Abuse

Many youth who have been sexually abused report, "I didn't know this shouldn't be happening." It's logical that most kids grow up believing the way things go in their homes and in their lives is the norm. By providing information to youth and adults on sexual abuse we give people the language they need to explain what may be going on in an unspoken part of their lives. Contact local agencies that specialize in abuse prevention to see if they can do a training session for adults/staff and have suggestions for posters, lesson plans, and speakers who can talk with teens. Provide all adults, guardians, and staff with copies of the What to Do if You Suspect Sexual Abuse handout in this chapter.

Refer to the resource section of this chapter for specific ideas.

If You Suspect Sexual Abuse

Your agency, professional license, and state or provincial laws will define your responsibility when you suspect someone is being sexually abused. See the section entitled "Know When and How to Report to Child Protective Services" on page 90 in the chapter on Physical Abuse for a discussion of how and when abuse must be reported, and your responsibilities as a reporter of abuse. The recommendations here are general guidelines for anyone who suspects sexual abuse.

Report your suspicion of sexual abuse immediately. Many professions require you to report suspicions of abuse immediately. Consult with your supervisor when appropriate, and contact your local Child Protective Services agency and file a report; see the Physical Abuse chapter for further information on filing a child protection report.

> "I wanted to keep it a secret because I didn't want pity. I was also scared of people's reactions. I blamed myself for the sexual abuse and I didn't tell because I didn't know what I wanted from people."
> —Sean

Don't force a disclosure. As difficult as this may be, let the teen determine when she discloses sexual abuse. Ask direct questions about your concerns with plenty of time for the adolescent to talk. Be clear, direct, nonjudgmental, and gentle with your concerns, and give examples of why you are concerned. Enter into the conversation without a predetermined outcome: don't assume the teen will disclose.

A relationship and environment that are caring and nonjudgmental lend themselves to a youth's feeling more able to disclose sexual abuse. While it's important to be on high alert with your suspicion, refrain from making the teen feel like the criminal through interrogative questioning.

Be calm. If you have suspicion of or if a teen discloses sexual abuse, refrain from exhibiting your anger/disgust/panic around the youth. Staying calm, being supportive, and maintaining a nonjudgmental stance are some of the most important things you can do to support someone who has been sexually abused. Your reaction to a youth's disclosure of sexual abuse can impact how he reacts to and understands the trauma. You want a teen to know that this is very serious, but you do not want to send a message that sexual abuse is something he cannot recover from.

Allow the teen to lead. We may feel compelled to ask a teen all of the questions we have, but that may be more to meet our own emotional needs than hers. Rather, refraining from asking many questions allows the youth to set the pace of the conversation(s). It is tremendously courageous for a teen to disclose any form of abuse; let her know how strong she is.

Believe what he says. Youth almost never lie about sexual abuse. Even if it feels horrible to wrap your mind around what a teen is saying, believe him.

Assure the youth this is not her fault. While it may seem obvious to us that a youth, or any human being, never deserves abuse, many victims of abuse believe they are to blame. The abuser may have told her she brought the abuse upon herself. Through persuasion by the abuser and/or messages we receive about abuse through media and culture, teens often believe they brought the abuse upon themselves. State as often as needed that abuse is a choice made by the abuser, and assure them they are not to blame and nothing they ever did is the cause for sexual abuse.

Do not blame the victim. We receive many victim-blaming messages in our society, such as the myth that girls who dress and act in a provocative manner are asking for the sexual attention of older men. Challenge yourself to explore any beliefs you are holding about a teen inviting sexual abuse. Do you believe a teen could cause sexual abuse through his dress or behavior? Do you believe teens should accept some responsibility for sexual abuse? Members of our society are expected to control and be responsible for their own behavior. No one causes sexual abuse but perpetrators.

Refer the youth to a counselor. Ideally, the decision to work with a counselor should be up to the youth. We can become overwhelmed with a desire to provide therapeutic help for teens, but if you are not a therapist, don't attempt to do so yourself. Just knowing of resources available in your community—particularly those agencies that specialize in abuse—and sharing this information is vital. Provide adolescents with information without pressuring them into counseling. The best work done in counseling is when it is the client's choice to seek help. If a teen asks for help, commit yourself to getting her help.

Affirm thoughts and feelings. There is no one right way to deal with abuse. Familiarize yourself with the common thoughts and feelings associated with sexual abuse, such as fear, guilt, embarrassment, anxiety, and anger. Share with the young person that his thoughts and feelings are a normal response to abuse. Acknowledge the way he feels and thinks, and reiterate that the way he may be feeling and thinking does not necessary equate with who he is. For example, if a teen says he believes he is "damaged goods," point out that this is a thought, and it does not mean that he *is* damaged goods.

Don't make promises you can't keep. While this may seem simple enough, the pain of hearing a teen share that she is being or has been sexually abused will naturally lend itself to our wanting to ensure it never happens again. Be careful to avoid statements like, "I will make sure this never happens to you again." You can play a powerful role in helping a teen who has been sexually abused, but you cannot guarantee perfect results in a sexual abuse case. Find out how sexual abuse cases are generally handled through the courts and child protective service agencies to better learn how you fit into this system.

RESOURCES

National Child Traumatic Stress Network (nctsnet.org). Provides resources and information for parents, caregivers, educators, and professionals on child traumatic stress.

National Sexual Assault Hotline: 800-656-HOPE. Free, confidential, available 24 hours a day.

RAINN: Rape, Abuse and Incest National Network (rainn.org).

Toni Cavanagh Johnson, Ph.D (tcajohn.com). Her books and pamphlets can be ordered from her Web site.

Don't Tell: The Sexual Abuse of Boys by Michel Dorais; translated by Isabel Denholm Meyer. Montreal: McGill-Queen's University Press, 2002.

Invisible Girls: The Truth about Sexual Abuse—A Book for Teen Girls, Young Women, and Everyone Who Cares about Them by Patty Feuereisen and Caroline Pincus. Emeryville, CA: Seal Press, 2005.

The Me Nobody Knows: A Guide for Teen Survivors by Barbara Bean and Shari Bennett. New York: Lexington Books, 1993.

Speak, DVD, directed by Jessica Sharzer (2003; Showtime Entertainment, 2005).

NOTES

1. J. Briere and D. M. Eliot, "Prevalence and Psychological Sequelae of Self-Reported Childhood Physical and Sexual Abuse in a General Population Sample of Men and Women," *Child Abuse and Neglect: The International Journal* 27 (2003): 1205–1222.

2. American Psychological Association Online. "Understanding Child Sexual Abuse: Education, Prevention, and Recovery," 2001, www.apa.org/releases/sexabuse/ (accessed September 24, 2007).

3. Rape and Abuse Crisis Center of Fargo/Moorhead. "Indicators of Child Sexual Abuse" (2003). Booklet. N.p.

What to Do if You Suspect Sexual Abuse

Report your suspicion of sexual abuse immediately. Contact your local Child Protective Services agency and file a report. Consult with your supervisor if appropriate.

Don't force a disclosure. As difficult as this may be, let the youth determine when he will disclose sexual abuse.

Be calm. If you have suspicion of or a teen discloses sexual abuse, refrain from exhibiting your anger/disgust/panic around the youth. Staying calm, being supportive, and maintaining a nonjudgmental stance are some of the most important things you can do to support someone who has been sexually abused.

Believe what she says. Youth rarely lie about sexual abuse.

Assure the youth this is not his fault. State as often as needed that abuse is a choice made by the abuser. Assure the teen he is not to blame and nothing he ever did is the cause for sexual abuse.

Don't blame the victim. Reaffirm to yourself that no one invites abuse, regardless of her appearance or behavior. Abuse is a choice made by the abuser.

Refer the youth to a counselor. Provide teens with referral information for counselors who specialize in sexual abuse. If a teen asks for help, commit yourself to getting him help.

Affirm her thoughts and feelings. No matter how she responds to the abuse, be considerate and supportive of her emotional state. Let her know that her thoughts and feelings are a normal response.

Don't make promises you can't keep. You can play a powerful role in helping a teen who has been sexually abused, but you cannot guarantee perfect results in a sexual abuse case. Learn how sexual abuse cases are generally handled through the courts and child protective services to better learn how you fit into this system.

SUICIDE

Suicide is a critical issue for teens. Completing suicide, attempting suicide, being exposed to suicidal behavior, and thoughts about suicide are all different ways teens might be affected by suicide.

Suicide is the third-leading cause of death for adolescents and young adults in the United States.[1] Only accidents and homicides happen more often than suicide. There is some debate about whether the rate of suicide is actually higher than reported because many suicides are reported as accidents, especially when it is unclear whether or not the person intended to kill himself. It is believed that most teen suicides occur at home after school.[2]

Suicide accounts for almost 13 percent of deaths among people ages 15 to 24 in the United States. Each year, there are about 10 suicides for every 100,000 young people—on average, about 12 suicides a day. Students across the United States were surveyed; in 2005, almost 17 percent of students in grades 9 to 12 had seriously considered suicide in the previous 12 months. Among these students, 22 percent were girls and 12 percent were boys. Many students acted on these thoughts: 8.4 percent of these students reported that they had made a suicide attempt in the year prior; 2.3 percent of the students reported that their suicide attempt was serious enough to require medical attention.[3]

What Are Suicidal Behaviors?

Suicidal behaviors include using firearms, cutting wrists, overdosing on drugs, and suffocation. The most common fatal suicide method is the use of firearms, but suffocation is being increasingly used.[4] Some suicide attempts may result in serious injuries, such as broken bones, brain damage, and organ damage. Some attempts may result in less serious physical injuries, but any attempt at suicide should be taken very seriously.

People who cut or burn themselves as a way to cope with their emotions are not necessarily engaging in suicidal behavior. Self-injury or self-harming behaviors may not be suicidal, but they are serious gestures that indicate the teen probably needs your help. For more information on self-injury, see page 101.

What Puts Youth at Risk for Suicide?

Certain factors put a teen at an increased risk for suicidal behaviors, and if you see any of these factors, it is important to help the teen and possibly refer him for professional help. Teens with a mental illness are at a greater risk for attempting suicide, and these illnesses may not be as obvious as the physical scars left by suicide attempts. Teens who use or abuse drugs or alcohol are at an increased risk for suicidal behavior; you should pay particular attention if the teen is increasing the amounts of drugs and alcohol he is consuming.

Teens who have impulsive or aggressive behaviors or who have frequent angry outbursts may also be at risk for attempting suicide. Others at risk are those who have recently experienced a loss or a stressful event, such as family problems, struggling with sexual orientation, an unexpected pregnancy, or the death of a loved one. It is sometimes difficult for teens to see that feelings about issues may pass or change over time, and they may be convinced that things will always be as bad as they seem at that moment. Having a previous suicide attempt also puts someone at an increased risk for committing suicide. Other risk factors include feeling alone, a physical illness, or problems with peers. This list is not inclusive, and it is important to remember that anyone might be thinking of suicide.

Warning Signs of Suicide

The American Association of Suicidology reports that as many as 80 percent of people who attempt or complete a suicide exhibited warning signs of the attempt.[5] A person who is considering suicide often talks about committing suicide or dying. She may mention that things would be easier if she just committed suicide or may say things like, "People would be better off if I weren't around." A person who is considering suicide may also undergo changes in appetite and sleep patterns. She may not be as interested in food as she once was. She may be sleeping excessively or having trouble falling or staying asleep. She may lose interest in personal hygiene or in her appearance. A teen who is thinking about committing suicide may also withdraw from friends and have no desire to socialize. She may take part in risky behaviors like drinking excessively, doing drugs, or driving too fast. She may give away her cherished or favorite possessions. If you see any of these behaviors in a teen, it is important to intervene and find out what is going on.

WHAT YOU CAN DO TO HELP

Be a Resource

Suicide is often preventable. Many people who attempt or complete a suicide have a mental illness, such as depression. Often the mental illness is not treated. It is imperative that any teen who is struggling with poor mental health get help from caring adults and mental health professionals, such as counselors.

Talking and listening are simple first steps toward preventing suicide. If you have concerns about a teen or see any of the warning signs of suicide, simply talking to the teen is a good way to help. Communicating that you care for him and are concerned for his safety lets him know that he is not alone.

> "When I planned my suicide and got ready to do it, the images of people who cared about me stopped me." —Jeremiah

Making suicide education materials available and visible may give a teen access to help when she is afraid to talk to an adult face-to-face. Post the numbers to suicide hotlines and educational materials where teens can see them and easily access them. It is important not only that adults know the warning signs of suicide but that teens know them as well. Teens will talk to each other about their feelings, and friends may be more attuned to changes in mood.

Speak Directly and Openly

There are many things you can do to help a teen who is thinking about suicide. One of the biggest myths about suicide is that bringing up the topic plants the idea in his head and increases the chance that he will commit suicide. The most important thing to remember about communicating with someone who is thinking of suicide is to speak directly with him about what he is experiencing. If you see any of the warning signs listed in this chapter or have other concerns about a teen, talk to him.

The first thing to do when you have concerns about a teen is to ask her directly if she is thinking about killing herself. Don't use words like "hurt yourself" or "go away" because these may not be clear. Ask, "Are you thinking about killing yourself?" Many people who are contemplating suicide are willing to talk about it. Just initiating the conversation is a good way to begin. It may help someone feel less alone just knowing that you are willing to talk to her about her thoughts and feelings. It also gets the issue out in the open so it can be addressed and help can be sought.

Once the issue is open for discussion, the next step is to listen. This may be harder than it sounds. People are often tempted to give the suicidal person reasons he should not kill himself. This is not listening—this is talking! *Listen* to what the teen has to say about how he is feeling and why he is feeling that way. Don't chastise him for feeling this way. The feelings he is experiencing are very real and need to be validated. When you do talk, let him know you care and that you are there for him.

There *are* some things you should avoid saying when having a conversation with a teen about suicide. Don't minimize her feelings—there are things that a teen might find devastating that you don't consider a big deal. Teen and adult brains work very differently; if a teen tells you she is despondent or angry about a situation, believe her. Don't say phrases like "You have everything to live for" or "Don't be silly—things aren't that bad" or "You're young—you'll get over this." Saying things like this minimizes the pain the teen is feeling and can make her feel worse. Instead, say, "It sounds like you are hurting quite a bit" or "I can see that you are very sad about this." It is important to offer support and remind her that there are people who love and want to help her.

Get Professional Help

It is important for a suicidal teen to get professional help. If it is a crisis and the teen says she is going to kill herself immediately, or refuses to stay and talk to you and you are afraid she is going to kill herself, call 911. If she is having thoughts of suicide, but has no plan to do so immediately, get her to a mental health professional as soon as possible. Call a counseling center or go to the emergency room. Be clear that the teen is thinking about killing herself, and these professionals will help guide you with the next steps to take. Do not leave the teen alone if you think the threat of suicide is immediate.

There are good questions to ask to assess the seriousness of the situation. Find out how long and how often he has been thinking of suicide. Ask him

how he would kill himself. If he has a plan for how he will do it, the risk is higher that he will attempt or complete a suicide. If his method of killing himself is more lethal, the risk he will die is greater (a highly lethal means of suicide is using a firearm; a less lethal means of suicide is taking pills). You should also consider whether the teen has access to his suicide method of choice, especially if he mentions a gun. If the teen is living with you, remove all possible means of suicide from the home. Remove ropes, belts, guns, pills, knives, and other sharp objects such as razors. A plan to commit suicide, no matter what the means or how lethal the means, is serious and should not be taken lightly.

What If There Is a Suicide in the School or Community?

When a teen commits suicide, there can be a ripple effect felt throughout the school and the community. When this type of event happens, it is important that the school and community be prepared to address it. Many schools are implementing crisis plans that can be used to help students after the suicide of a peer. If your school or organization has such a plan, make sure you know what your role is in a crisis. If your school or organization has no plan, you should seek advice from professionals about how one can be implemented.

Youth may react to news of a suicide in several different ways, but many young people may experience behavioral and emotional reactions, even if they did not know the teen who completed suicide. After a crisis, you may observe extreme emotions, behavioral problems, and problems relating to others. You may also see extreme sadness, guilt, excessive worry, angry outbursts, or even a sudden lack of emotions. Some behavioral problems may include copycat suicide behavior, eating problems, using drugs and alcohol, violent outbursts, staying at home, or isolation. Teens may also have problems relating to others in the wake of a tragic event. They may fight more, become clingy, or avoid their friends or families.

Working together with the school, organization, or community is important when trying to ease the problems that follow a suicide. It is also important to acknowledge that pain may be felt for months after a suicide. Many people follow up with teens in the days after a suicide, but maintaining this support for several months is vital to a comprehensive crisis plan. As an individual, one of the best things you can do is use your strength-based interviewing skills when talking to teens you are concerned about.

RESOURCES

American Association of Suicidology: Dedicated to the Understanding and the Prevention of Suicide (suicidology.org).

Kidshealth.org: About Teen Suicide (kidshealth.org/parent/emotions/behavior/suicide.html).

National Hopeline Network. Phone: 800-SUICIDE.

National Suicide Prevention Lifeline. Phone: 800-723-TALK.

National Youth Crisis Hotline. Phone: 800-442-HOPE.

Suicide Prevention Resource Center (sprc.org).

NOTES

1. National Center for Injury Prevention and Control, "Fatal Injuries: Leading Causes of Death Reports" (Atlanta, GA: Centers for Disease Control and Prevention, 2006).

2. American Association of Suicidology, "Youth Suicide Fact Sheet," www.suicidology.org/associations/1045/files/Youth2004.pdf (accessed October 4, 2007).

3. D. K. Eaton, L. Kann, S. Kinchen, J. Ross, J. Hawkins, W. A. Harris, et al., "Youth Risk Behavior Surveillance: United States, 2005," *Journal of School Health* 76 (2006): 353–372.

4. American Association of Suicidology, "Youth Suicide Fact Sheet."

5. Ibid.

Warning Signs of Suicide

- Talking about or mentioning suicide

- Preoccupation with death or dying

- Saying things like "I'd be better off dead"

- Having depression or another mental illness

- Being very sad for a time, and then suddenly seeming happy and at peace

- Giving away favorite possessions

- Drastic changes in behavior

- Mood swings or angry outbursts

- Withdrawing from friends and social activities

- Participating in risky behaviors like excessive drinking or dangerous driving

- Changes in sleeping or eating patterns

What to Do If You Think Someone Is Suicidal

- Ask in a clear, concise manner if he is thinking of committing suicide

- Listen to her feelings

- Let him know you are there to listen

- Get help from a professional

- Don't leave her alone

- Find out if he has a plan for killing himself and ask what the plan is

- Acknowledge her pain: "I can see you are very upset right now"

- Don't talk down to him or make him feel guilty about being suicidal

- Remove pills, ropes, firearms, and knives from her access

APPENDIX

MORE WAYS YOU CAN MAKE A DIFFERENCE

This book discusses issues that often result in significant difficulties for teens—and a great many of these issues stem from social and systemic oppression. These challenges are much larger than the thoughts and behaviors of individuals; they arise in a society where certain groups dominate other groups, resulting in an imbalance of power. The dominant group receives unearned advantages and privileges, while the subordinate group experiences oppression, discrimination, and prejudice. (If you belong to a "dominant" group, that doesn't mean that *you* misuse your power and privileges, but rather that they result from an imbalance of power.)

Racism, classism, sexism, heterosexism, and ableism are all examples of oppression that stems from an imbalance of power in social groups. These adversities create enormous barriers that many youth face, and the stress and pressure of these adversities can exacerbate other difficulties a teen is experiencing.

WHAT YOU CAN DO TO HELP

It is impossible to adequately address injustice in a few paragraphs, but utilize these suggestions as a starting point.

Understand the Terminology

A good way to begin is to share common definitions of these issues with the team you work with, and spread your understanding of the issues into your larger community. Gloria Yamato defines oppression as "the systematic, institutionalized mistreatment of one group of people by another for whatever reason."[1] If we carry her definition of oppression into our understanding of the issues, which are rooted in oppression and privilege, then racism is the systematic, institutionalized mistreatment of people based on their skin color and other physical characteristics; sexism is the systematic, institutionalized mistreatment of women based on their sex, and so on.

The following are also important terms to understand:

Bias: an inclination or preference either for or against an individual or group that interferes with impartial judgment.

Culture: the patterns of daily life learned consciously and unconsciously by a group of people. These patterns can be seen in language, governing practices, arts, customs, holiday celebrations, food, religion, dating rituals, and clothing, to name a few examples.

Discrimination: the denial of justice and fair treatment by both individuals and institutions in many arenas, including employment, education, and housing. Discrimination is an action that can follow prejudiced thinking.

Prejudice: prejudging, making a decision about a person or a group of people without sufficient knowledge. Prejudicial thinking is frequently based in stereotypes.

Stereotype: an oversimplified generalization about a person or group of people without regard for individual differences.[2]

Influence Others

However you choose your methods of ongoing education, whether it is through trainings, readings, or seminars, reach out to others and encourage them to become involved in learning more. As you learn more, talk with your family and friends about what you've learned. Involve the teens you work with in standing against injustice. For example, collaborate on specific projects with agencies in your community that work to end injustice, create a social justice committee for your program and actively recruit representation on the committee from all groups of people. The opportunities we have to combat injustice are limitless.

Advocate for Inclusive Resources

Assess the resources (books, curriculum guides, music) you use in your home and at work. Are they sensitive to multiculturalism? Do they offer many worldviews and perspectives on life? Follow the recommendations of Emily Style, who writes, "All students deserve a curriculum which mirrors their own experience back to them, upon occasion—thus validating it in the public world of the school. But curriculum must also insist upon the fresh air of windows into the experience of others—who also need and deserve the public validation of the school curriculum."[3] Provide both windows and mirrors to everyone through your resources. Encourage your program or supervisor to utilize agency dollars in a way that represents all people.

Encourage Your Agency to Examine Itself

You have the opportunity to create a great force for social change if you can involve your agency in examining its biases and working toward being more inclusive. Are there things in your program that are getting in the way of talking about injustice? Do your leadership and stakeholders reflect both your mission and diverse groups? For example, if you work with people in poverty, are there leaders in your organization who can give an authentic voice to this experience? If not, what does the agency need to do to welcome authentic voices? Are you providing leadership and membership opportunities to all? What can you do to recruit more people from diverse groups? How can your agency work with leaders in social justice to help your agency change?

Social Activism in Your Classroom or Youth Group

- Implement a zero-tolerance rule in your classroom, workplace, or center. Do not allow abusive language or behaviors.

- Start educating youth about abuse at a young age. Curriculum for youth of all ages is available through Red Flag Green Flag Resources (redflaggreenflag.com).

- Implement curricula or programming specific to teen dating violence. An outstanding resource for handouts and resources is loveisnotabuse.com.

- Facilitate a drug education workshop in your school. Training resources and information about such workshops (such as the DVD "Safety First: The Workshop") are available at safety1st.org.

- Engage your school/youth group in homelessness awareness. Invite staff from your local homeless shelters to speak with your group on their program and homelessness. Coordinate a student-organized collection drive for area shelters that reflect their current needs (hygiene supplies, towels).

- Incorporate GLBTQ issues and authors into your classroom or organization. Specific lesson plans are available at advocatesforyouth.org. Click on "Lesson Plans."

- Incorporate Child Abuse Prevention Month (April) into your lesson plans. You can download a community resource packet filled with ideas to promote protective factors that reduce the risk of child abuse and to raise awareness from the Prevent Child Abuse Web site, preventchildabuse.org/publications/cap/index/shtml.

- Engage your school/youth group in National Foster Care Awareness Month every May. Invite staff from your local social service agency to speak with your group about their program and the needs of youth in their care.

Social Activism in Your Program

- Be a leader in your agency by advocating for a policy mandating that all people who come into contact with youth have complete background checks prior to involvement with your program.

- Invite a spokesperson from a domestic violence program to speak to employees over a lunch hour.

- Ask your Human Resources department to include information in a staff memo, e-mail, or other communication about counseling benefits that are available to people being abused.

- Organize your workplace in a "Take Back the Night" rally. Contact your local domestic violence program for information. Information is also available at takebackthenight.org.

- Work for antidiscrimination policies in your organization. Check to see if your workplace includes GLBTQ people in its antidiscrimination policies. If it doesn't, work toward their inclusion and use opportunities to educate gatekeepers and other staff on the importance of protecting everyone's rights. Specific

information is available at the Gay, Lesbian, and Straight Education Network Web site (glsen.org).

Social Activism in the Community

- Get involved in protecting the after-school activities for teens in your community, particularly in rural settings where there are fewer resources for teens. One of the many benefits of extracurricular programs is the safe haven they provide for teens from abusive homes and relationships.

- Become part of or start public forums on all forms of child abuse in your community.

- Volunteer. Most agencies have an array of needs you can match your strengths to.

- Get involved in promoting and providing positive parenting skills and courses in your community.

- Join your local Homeless Coalition. If you work with youth experiencing homelessness, encourage leadership opportunities for these youth on the coalition's board and committees.

- Volunteer at a local food pantry or shelter and bring a friend.

Social Activism in the Government

- Contact your state representatives and let them know you support tougher sentences for perpetrators of sexual abuse, physical abuse, and domestic violence.

- Contact your members of Congress and urge more federal funding for domestic violence programs and abuse prevention programs.

- Look into how your state's laws relate to teen dating violence. Contact Break the Cycle (310-286-3383 or info@breakthecycle.org) for help in taking action to improve the laws in your state.

- Become involved in the Universal Living Wage campaign for fair wages (universallivingwage.org).

- Support the Bringing America Home Act, a bill designed to end homelessness in our country through housing, health, economic, and civil rights (bringingamericahome.org).

- Join the Human Rights Campaign. This civil rights organization works to achieve GLBT equality (hrc.org).

Be Patient with Yourself and with Change

Try not to be too impatient with yourself, others, and social change. The process of unlearning and relearning the way power, justice, and injustice operate is long; give yourself time, give others time, and recognize that if social injustice is rooted in our systems and institutions, social change will be a slow process. Find small ways to be involved in larger efforts to dismantle injustice, especially when you feel frustrated.

NOTES

1. G. Yamato, "Something about the Subject Makes It Hard to Name," in *Changing Our Power: An Introduction to Women Studies*, ed. J. W. Cochran, D. Langston, and C. Woodward (Dubuque, IA: Kendall/Hunt Publishing Company, 1991), 7–10.

2. Anti-Defamation League and Barnes & Noble, *Close the Book on Hate: 101 Ways to Combat Prejudice* (New York: ADL's New England Regional Office Staff, 2001).

3. E. Style, "Curriculum as Window and Mirror," in *Seeding the Process of Multicultural Education*, ed. C. L. Nelson and K. A. Wilson (Plymouth: Minnesota Inclusiveness Program, 1998), 149–156.

THE DEVELOPMENTAL ASSETS PROFILE (DAP)

AN ASSESSMENT FOR INDIVIDUALS OR SMALL GROUPS

Based on Search Institute's Developmental Assets framework, the Developmental Assets Profile (DAP) provides a quick, simple, valid, and reliable self-report of a young person's view of the world. In addition, it allows you to document, quantify, and portray adolescents' reports of the types and levels of assets working in their lives—a 360-degree look at a teen's internal and external assets—and gives you a valuable look into the positive development of an individual young person or group of youth.

The DAP can be administered on paper or as a Web-based application. The Web-based option provides a secure environment in which to administer, score, view, print, store, and export DAP results.

The DAP is ideal for:

- **Individual assessments** by qualified clinicians, school counselors, mental health practitioners, and social workers; and
- **Group assessments** for youth programs in schools, juvenile justice, mental health, and family services settings.

For further details, call Search Institute's Survey Services at 800-888-7828 or go to search-institute .org/surveys.

ABOUT THE AUTHORS

Jill Nelson, Ph.D., is an assistant professor in the counseling program at North Dakota State University in Fargo. She coordinates the community counseling program and has been a Nationally Certified Counselor (NCC) since 1998. She has experience counseling children, teens, adults, and families. Her favorite people to work with are teens facing tough times, and most of her professional counseling experience is in working with teens in both inpatient and outpatient settings. She obtained her B.A. in psychology and German and her master's degree in counseling from the University of South Dakota. She received her Ph.D. in counselor education and supervision from Kent State University.

Sarah Kjos, M.Ed., has spent the last 12 years working with children and adolescents facing tough experiences, first as a case manager and advocate for homeless families and youth in shelter and school-based settings, and now as a counselor at the Rape & Abuse Crisis Center of Fargo, providing individual and group counseling to child and adult survivors of sexual abuse, sexual assault, and domestic violence. She obtained her undergraduate degree in sociology from Moorhead State University, and earned a master's degree in counseling from North Dakota State University. She lives in Moorhead, Minnesota, with her daughters and husband.

more great books

FROM SEARCH INSTITUTE PRESS

SAFE PLACES TO LEARN
21 Lessons to Help Students Promote a Caring School Climate

by Paul Sulley, Search Institute Trainer

Teachers, administrators, coaches, counselors, and other caring adults involved in education will get the tools they need (including step-by-step lessons, relevant and thoughtful discussion questions, and plenty of reproducibles) to help students create a safe, caring, asset-building learning climate. This book is not just for brick and mortar schools—all learning environments, including community programs, juvenile justice programs, and alternative schools will benefit from the 21 lessons.

Peer leadership is the key component in this timely book. Research proves that giving young people the ability to be change makers—complementing their own, as well as their peers' school experience—is an effective solution to the ongoing "bullying" problem facing administrators and educators.

$29.95; 140 pages; softcover (includes CD-ROM); 8½" x 11"

THE BEST OF BUILDING ASSETS TOGETHER
Favorite Group Activities That Help Youth Succeed

by Jolene L. Roehlkepartain

From physically challenging to thought-provoking, engaging to reflective, this book offers a creative vehicle for studying topics such as leadership, diversity, and community involvement (among others), and allows team leaders to empower young people to discover their own strengths. Includes real-world tips from educators and youth providers and a CD-ROM with over 50 reproducible handouts in English and Spanish.

$34.95; 160 pages; softcover (includes CD-ROM); 8½" x 11"

TEACHING KIDS TO CHANGE THE WORLD
Lessons to Inspire Social Responsibility For Grades 6-12

by Jennifer Griffin-Wiesner, M.Ed., and Chris Maser, M.S.

Not just another social action or service project how-to book, this supplemental educational resource helps adults teach young people *how* to think about a broad range of social issues, not just what to think about them. Thematic lessons and inspired examples help students in grades 6–12 comprehend long-term change and the costs of sustainability.

$24.95; 104 pages; softcover; 8½" x 11"

150 WAYS TO SHOW KIDS YOU CARE POSTER

Discover 150 great ideas to make kids feel special every day. This bright mini-poster lists thoughtful and practical little acts of love and caring that make a world of difference to young people. This foldable mini-poster should be on every bulletin board and refrigerator! It's also perfect for companies to spread the word by inserting in mailings and employee information envelopes.

$11.95 (pack of 20); coated paper; folded: 5½" x 3¾"; unfolds to a 5½" x 34" poster

PASS IT ON!
Ready-to-Use Handouts for Asset Builders

Anyone can spread practical and easy ideas quickly, inexpensively, and effectively with this set of handout masters. Geared for any audience, the 90 reproducible handouts include an introduction to Developmental Assets, ideas for individuals and groups, tools for community initiatives, and tips on

using books, videos, and magazines to build assets. 10 Spanish handouts and one French handout included! A section on grouping the handouts helps get the right information to the right groups. The CD-ROM features PDFs of all the handouts from the book.

$29.95; 176 pages; softcover (includes CD-ROM); 8½" x 11"

WHEN PARENTS ASK FOR HELP
Everyday Issues through an Asset-Building Lens

by Renie Howard

Each handout reframes an issue—curfews, homework, chores, dating, body image, conflicts, risky activities, fights, jobs, depression, and more—from an asset-based point of view. Parents and caregivers get plenty of encouragement, hope, and practical ideas with these reproducible articles that speak directly to the real dilemmas their adolescents face. Teachers, counselors, and staff at youth-serving organizations can use this resource to help parents build assets, not just solve problems.

$29.95; 144 pages; softcover; 8½" x 11"

AN ASSET BUILDER'S GUIDE TO TRAINING PEER HELPERS
Fifteen Sessions on Communication, Assertiveness, and Decision-Making Skills

by Barbara Varenhorst, Ph.D.

Young people can make a powerful difference in the lives of their peers. More often than not, youth turn to their friends for help, rather than to adults. This resource includes a comprehensive, 15-session curriculum that allows you to lead a peer-helping program full of activities to give young people the skills they need to build assets.

$39.95; 176 pages; softcover; 8½" x 11"

RAISE THEM UP:
The Real Deal on Reaching Unreachable Kids

by Kareem Moody with Anitra Budd

The dramatic, real-world experiences of hard-to-reach youth inspire these vivid and compelling essays on effectively connecting with disengaged children.

The jargon-free approach shows you how to intentionally engage kids and turn seemingly dire situations into inspirational success stories. Underlying each account is an emphasis on the need for a focused, ongoing dialogue with at-risk young people about their unique strengths and opportunities to grow up to be healthy, vibrant members of society.

$9.95; 112 pages; softcover; 5½" x 7½"

LIFE FREAKS ME OUT—AND THEN I DEAL WITH IT
(Reassuring Secrets from a Former Teenager)

by K. L. Hong

Turbulent. Exhilarating. Confusing. Real. These words describe what *Life Freaks Me Out* is all about—living, being, and growing up as a teen. Forget the fluff; this down-to-earth memoir touches on hard-hitting issues—drugs, alcohol, self-esteem, relationships, sex—to emphasize to today's teens the power of choice. Author K. L. Hong takes readers on a candid journey of her own teen years (and the years since), offering young people guidance on answering life's big questions.

$9.95; 168 pages; softcover; 5½" x 7½"

TAKE IT TO THE NEXT LEVEL
Making Your Life What You Want It to Be

by K. L. Hong

Created just for teens and young adolescents, *Take It to the Next Level* helps young people focus on their successes, explore what they really want and how to get it, and celebrate their efforts and accomplishments. Filled with activities and journal topics, this booklet guides young people through the journey of adolescence from a Developmental Assets approach.

$15.95 (pack of 20); 20 pages; booklet; 5½" x 8½"

GREAT GROUP GAMES
175 Boredom-Busting, Zero-Prep Team Builders for All Ages

by Susan Ragsdale and Ann Saylor

Great Group Games offers enjoyable games and activities that will gently disband group-busting cliques, help newcomers feel welcome, and turn your participants into friends who can count on each other. Authors Ragsdale and Saylor, experienced trainers and youth development leaders, have compiled games that are perfect for classrooms, retreats, workshops, and groups on the go. Each game includes details on timing, supplies, set up, suggested group size, game tips, and reflection questions. Best of all, the games are far from mindless. Games like "Tiny Teach," "Common Ground," and "The Winding Road" will really make your group members think. These low-prep activities work for small or large groups and can be done anywhere. You'll make every moment meaningful and every game great!

$16.95; 228 pages; softcover; 6" x 9"

CONVERSATIONS ON THE GO
Clever Questions to Keep Teens and Grown-Ups Talking

by Mary Ackerman

Looking for a fun way to encourage family and other youth-adult conversations? This book is filled with intriguing questions, some deep and some just fun, guaranteed to stretch the imagination and bring out each person's personality and true self. Adults and young people can take turns asking questions such as: Where do your ancestors come from? What does integrity mean to you? This stimulating, go-anywhere book gives teens and adults a chance to find out what the other thinks about the big questions and the little ones.

$9.95; 100 pages; softcover; 5½" x 5½"

POSITIVE VALUES CARDS

Teachers, counselors, and youth workers love to give their students these sturdy, credit-card-sized reminders of the positive values that should guide kids in life. One side lists six positive values, and the other side lists questions to help young people make reasonable choices.

$12.95 (pack of 20); plastic cards; 2¼" x 3½"

PERSONAL COMMITMENT CARDS

Personal Commitment Cards are perfect handouts for the young people in your life as reminders that they play an important role in the quality of their own lives. One side of the card states a personal affirmation and includes a signature bar for youth to sign their commitment to the statement. The other side lists asset actions the young person can commit to.

$12.95 (pack of 20); plastic cards; 2¼" x 3½"

MENTORING FOR MEANINGFUL RESULTS
Asset-Building Tips, Tools, and Activities for Youth and Adults

by Kristie Probst

Mentoring for Meaningful Results is a mentoring program leader's complete "start-up kit" that provides mentors, mentees, and parents or caregivers everything they need to establish and maintain a successful mentoring relationship. Using practical tips and activities along with the Developmental Assets framework, *Mentoring for Meaningful Results* will enhance mentoring programs in schools, organizations, and communities across the country, as well as the lives of the children and youth they serve.

$27.95; 120 pages; softcover; 8½" x 11"